Inside French Rugby

Inside French Rugby

Confessions of a Kiwi Mercenary

JOHN DANIELL

AWA PRESS

First edition published in 2007 by Awa Press, 16 Walter Street, Wellington, New Zealand.

National Library of New Zealand Cataloguing-in-Publication Data
Daniell, John, 1972-
Inside French rugby : confessions of a kiwi mercenary / John Daniell.
ISBN 978-0-9582750-1-9
1. Daniell, John, 1972- 2. Rugby Union football—France.
I. Title.
796.3330944—dc 22

Internal design and typesetting by Jill Livestre, Archetype, Wellington
Printed by Printlink, Wellington
This book is typeset in Sabon and Helvetica Neue

www.awapress.com

About the author

John Daniell was born in New Zealand, and educated both there and in England. After studying English at Oxford University, he worked as a journalist for Radio New Zealand and Capital Television. His early rugby career included playing for England Schoolboys (1990), New Zealand Under 19s (1991), New Zealand Colts (1992), Marist St Pats (1992–97), Oxford University (Blue, 1992–94) and Wellington Lions (1994–96). In 1996 he turned professional, playing for French clubs Racing (1997–2000), Perpignan (2000–2003) and Montpellier Hérault (2003–2006). Currently a free-lance journalist, he has been published in *The Observer*, *The Sunday Telegraph* (UK), *The Evening Post*, *The New Zealand Listener*, and French publications *Rugby* and *La Semaine du Roussillon*. He lives in Montpellier, France with his girlfriend, Marion Chaulet. He has a daughter, Chloé.

Contents

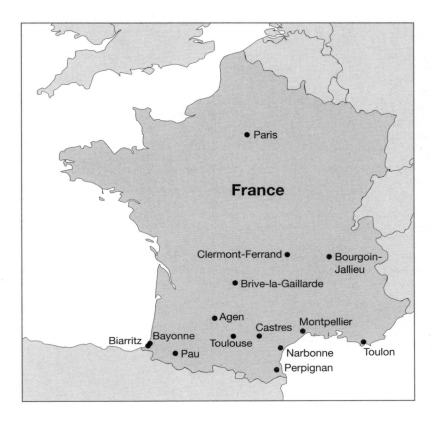

Agen . . . . Sporting Union Agen Lot et Garonne

Bayonne . . . . Aviron Bayonnais

Biarritz . . . . Biarritz Olympique

Bourgoin-Jallieu . . . . Club Sportif Bourgoin-Jallieu

Brive-la-Gaillarde . . . . Club Athlétique Brive Corrèze Limousin

Clermont-Ferrand . . . Association Sportive Montferrandaise Clermont
Auvergne (Montferrand)

Castres . . . . Castres Olympique

Montpellier . . . . Montpellier Hérault Rugby Club

Narbonne . . . . Racing Club Narbonne Méditerranée

Paris . . . . Stade Français

Pau . . . . Section Paloise

Perpignan . . . . Union Sportive Arlequins Perpignan

Toulon . . . . Rugby Club Toulonnais

Toulouse . . . . Stade Toulousain

Introduction

Mercenary' is not a pretty word. It sounds like a cold-eyed thug ready to change his loyalty for money. I am a mercenary, and so are most of my friends. If, as George Orwell said, serious sport is war minus the shooting, we are its soldiers, playing out make-believe conflicts in front of partisan crowds. We do this for money and for the love of the game, but mainly for the money.

As a rule we are known as professional rugby players. This is a bit like calling a spade a shovel: you could be forgiven for thinking they are the same thing, but if you have to actually work with one you soon see the difference. To understand what makes them different (professionals and mercenaries, not shovels and spades), you need to know about rugby.

These days rugby may look like an organised career move, but I fell into it for want of anything else to do. My degree in English literature hadn't proved to be the instant passport to a high-flying career in journalism I had hoped. I had done some work for a regional television station, but the station had quickly gone bust. After finishing a temporary job as assistant producer for Radio New Zealand's Morning Report, I was looking for something to turn my hand to.

Foreign shores looked attractive. Friends from university were fetched up in far-flung, exotic places such as Paris, Moscow and New York. I applied to the Australian High Commission for a job organising a forum in Nauru, a remote island with a population of 11,000 people and a landscape scarred by a century of phosphate mining. The job hadn't previously featured on my ideal career path, but I was gutted to miss out. Various other possibilities turned out to be dead-ends. I was stuck in the young person's Catch-22 where all jobs require experience and there is no way to acquire experience because you can't get a job.

And then rugby went professional. It felt like winning Lotto without even buying a ticket. At 24, I already had fifteen years' experience of the game, and given the limited time span of a rugby career I could even be said to be approaching my peak. Rather than struggling to get on to the bottom of the ladder in some other rat race, I could slot in somewhere in the middle of the newly created, and apparently relatively lucrative, rugby market.

Of course, no one starts out playing rugby because of money. Like any sport, you get into it because it looks like fun, or you are press-ganged by an overbearing father. As is often the case in New Zealand, I started playing at school. Wherever you start, part of rugby's attraction is the reassuring sense of belonging to something bigger than you. You make friends with team-mates, and have a role to play in a group that needs you to perform well. Representing your school or your club or your town against all comers, you share the joy of victory and the bitter taste of defeat, discover the benefits of hard work, learn how to complain about the referee and the unfairness of it all, and generally grow up.

So far, this is much like any other team sport. The magic of rugby, though, lies in its peculiar emphasis on two basic pillars—inclusiveness and interdependence. Compared to a relatively simple game such as soccer, rugby's rules are complex enough to need a variety of different body types and skills. In a rugby team there is a place for everyone: fat kids (or 'big-boned children', if their parents prefer) prop the scrum; the tall and ungainly like me are predestined to play lock; rangy, athletic types become loose forwards; the more dexterous, intelligent players run the game from the halfback positions; nimble runners find themselves in the outside backs. If you are scrawny, slow, dull-witted and uncoordinated, you may find your participation limited to bringing on the oranges at half-time; the writing is on the wall. You could always become a referee.

Put simply, the aim of a rugby team is to get hold of the ball, and to organise so that one player places the ball behind the goal-line to score a try. Equally important, of course, is preventing the opposition doing the same thing. All this requires teamwork, certain special skills and physical courage. I am not going to get involved in rules or tactics because that would take up a book in itself. Yes, you can kick the ball between the posts as well, but that isn't really the heart of the game. History buffs will tell you the reason a try is called a 'try' is that when the game was first played it was worth nothing: putting the ball behind the line merely gave you the chance to *try* for a shot at goal. But the game has moved on since then.

The nature of rugby as a contact sport—'collision sport' is perhaps more appropriate—means physical courage is important. In terms of injuries, rugby is right up there at the top of the table. Throwing yourself at someone running at full speed is, under normal circumstances, verging on the insane, and not something that comes naturally. For young men this is, of course, part of the attraction: the danger raises the stakes, and by facing up to it you get to prove to your peers that you are reliable and brave. Your mates have to prove themselves as well—each player must provide his own particular skills if the team is to be successful, and strong bonds of mutual respect soon form. The performance of the team becomes a source of pride, reinforcing the sense of belonging to the community. Rugby players—including women—are often seen as macho, and there is a pleasingly primal element to the game that appeals to unsophisticated but deeply rooted parts of our nature.

Rugby associates itself with old-fashioned values: virility, self-sacrifice and pride. One of the great rugby clichés is about having 'pride in the jersey'. I groan inwardly whenever I hear this, but it is a kind of shorthand for the bedrock on which the game is built. This is where mercenaries part company with professional rugby players. The idea behind having pride in the jersey is that when you pull on your team colours you are representing not only yourself, or you and your mates having a muddy-kneed run-around, but a whole community. You are supposed to feel a debt of honour to all those who have gone before you, and to the people who will be supporting you because you represent them. The French refer to this as *l'esprit de clocher*, which my dictionary bluntly defines as parochialism, but the sense is more romantic. Literally, a *clocher* is a church's clock tower. Symbolically, it stands for everything a good Frenchman holds close to his heart—his family, his friends, his town—the roots of an existence.

You can only really have pride in the jersey if the jersey, and what it stands for, mean something to you, otherwise it's just another jersey, black, white, red, blue, multicoloured or whatever. I spent three years at my secondary school in New Zealand thinking of the First XV as heroes, and then I became one of them. There was a purity and intensity to the thrill of playing for that team I have seldom felt since.

The biggest kick for a New Zealander, of course, is pulling on the black jersey. In 1992, I played for the New Zealand Under 21s against Australia. The night before the game my team-mate Mark Mayerhofler said we should be ready to die for the jersey. I can remember thinking this was a bit strong— but then he went on to be an All Black and I didn't. The next day, with 20 minutes to go, I comprehensively buggered my shoulder in a tackle. The other lock had already gone off so there were no more replacements, but I was really feeling it. The team physiotherapist had a look at my shoulder and said, 'The coach wants you to tough it out.'

This is the sort of thing young men dream of: twenty minutes to go, a hard-fought victory beckoning against the hated Australians in front of thousands of people, and New Zealand needs you to tough it out. But when you are actually on the field, unable to lift your arm because you feel as though you have been shot with an elephant gun, your thoughts run more along the lines of, 'Fuck this for a game of soldiers.' No one's paying you. There's every chance that if you keep playing the injury is going to get worse; at the very least it will hurt like hell at every moment of contact. But of course you stay on. It's New Zealand against Australia. Pride in the jersey. You love it, really.

If you think this sounds as though I am trying to present myself as a hero, you're probably right, although anyone else in the team would have done the same thing—in just the same way as we had all spent the long hours training and playing to get ourselves to a level of performance where we were good enough to be chosen for the national team. This was 1992, four years before rugby went professional. None of us imagined we might make money out of it. When I started playing for Wellington in 1994 it was the same thing—long hours of training, games eating up the weekends, and all for what?

In reality, there was a raft of different reasons for participation. Playing for a top team conferred social status. You had the opportunity to prove yourself, and enjoy the fun and the camaraderie of team spirit. And there was the sheer pleasure of doing something well. But at bottom there was one thing that justified all the necessary energy and drive and ambition and—although the wholesome idealism of it pains my cynical soul—it was pride in the jersey.

Finally, in 1996, we started getting paid: we became professional rugby players. At first this didn't seem to change anything. We were still playing for the same team. The training hours were the same (we didn't make enough to give up our jobs). We just got a cheque at the end of the month.

But then things did change. That season I had what I can best describe as a 'complicated' relationship with the Wellington coach, Frank Walker. At the beginning of the season he asked me to captain the side. I felt this was a bad idea—I was inexperienced, and there were plenty of players better qualified for the job. However, being a sucker for flattery, I allowed myself to be persuaded to take the less glamorous, but equally less onerous, role of vice-captain. Then, after a good series of wins, we lost one game, and as we were going into the changing-room for the next game Frank sent the team manager to tell me that it wasn't worth my while getting changed: I was being dumped.

My chances of a Super 12 contract—a full-time professional salary—for the coming season instantly went west. But if I looked hard enough there was an upside: although I no longer had any hope of fulfilling my ambition of playing for Wellington in the Super 12, I was also free of the emotional and contractual ties that had bound me to my home town.

Before the advent of professional rugby, a player played for the team in the town where he lived. You lived in that town because you worked or studied there, or simply because you were brought up there and it never occurred to you to move.

In any case, you made it your home for reasons other than rugby. However, the arrival of professionalism meant you could choose a team (providing they would have you) and that team's hometown would become your home: all you had to do was play rugby for them.

Of course, this meant 'pride in the jersey' went out the window. You could find yourself wearing colours that meant nothing at all, alongside team-mates you didn't know and who didn't speak the same language as you, in a town you previously didn't even know existed. You would be doing this because the team's management had agreed to pay you a sum of money large enough to make you want to move there and run around doing all the things that you used to do for love and not for money. You would have become a mercenary, like me.

Having decided I was fresh out of rugby-playing luck at home, I went to England and had an interview with Dick Best, director of rugby at Harlequins. He said some nice things and offered me £20,000 a year, plus a £1000-a-game win-bonus for all championship games, including the Anglo-Welsh league. All up, it amounted to around £30,000 a year. As this was about NZ$90,000, and considerably more than a Super 12 contract, it looked pretty sweet, although I later found out that I could have hoped for more. Some crazy figures were flying around in the early days of profession-alism in England.

I had a similar interview at the London Wasps Rugby Club with Nigel Melville, who said much the same things and came up with much the same offer, contingent on my getting a work permit. This quickly became the sticking point. In order to play in England, you had to have a British passport or have played for your country in the last 18 months, in which case you were considered expert enough to be able to pass on useful pointers to your team-mates—although, as there was no distinction made between playing for New Zealand or Croatia at international level, this was a bit of a loophole.

Meeting neither of these criteria, I left for France, where clubs were then allowed two foreign players, and found myself in contract negotiations in a smoky room just outside Paris with Christophe Mombet, the coach of Racing Club. Racing, Mombet said, usually paid players between 5000 and 10,000 francs a month. It was a pittance compared to what the English clubs were offering, but they would throw in accommodation as well. I said I wouldn't come for less than 10,000, there were smiles all round (damn, I obviously went too low), a handshake and the deal was done.

If this sounds like a bleak story of a wayward young man selling his soul for a few dollars, of the corrupting power of market forces, and of the road to disillusion with a once pure and noble sport, well yes, there is an element of that. As singer Cyndi Lauper pointed out, 'Money changes everything.' But there are plenty of upsides. Rugby's global marketplace gives players the opportunity to see different cultures from the inside and make new friends, while being well paid to do what we love.

There is something of a French Foreign Legion flavour to a team made up of individuals from so many disparate backgrounds: Montpellier, the club for which I was playing when the events described in this book took place, has, as well as New Zealanders, Georgians, South Africans, Samoans, a Muslim and a Jew, an Englishman and an Argentinian, all united for a common cause. And while the relationship between a player and his new club seems more of an arranged marriage than a love match, over time the right amount of goodwill on both sides can lead to it becoming highly beneficial for all concerned. For all the martial metaphors, poorly controlled aggression and bloodthirsty crowds, serious sport, if it is warlike, is, crucially, *minus* the shooting.

The truth is that the lot of the rugby mercenary is hard to beat, and the rich rugby culture of France is as good a place as any to get your knees muddy and your hands dirty. My grandfather spent a few years on the fields of France wearing the drab khaki of our country's colours in World War I, and God knows we have it sweet compared to his generation.

When I signed up to play rugby in France, the flow of players from New Zealand was just a trickle. Today it is more like a flood, as top All Blacks such as Tana Umaga and Byron Kelleher take advantage of the spoils to be had from donning French club jerseys. This is one of the great sea changes of rugby in our time, with revolutionary implications for the game not only in the southern hemisphere but around the world. Unless you are a power-broker at the IRB or a big wheel in a national union, whether or not it is good for rugby is a moot point: it's happening, and we had better get used to it.

Montpellier, Chez Moi

This is my third season playing for Montpellier, a medium-sized town—about 200,000 people, swelling to 400,000 if you count the outlying agglomeration—in the south of France, a few miles inland from the Mediterranean, in the middle of the bulge of the gulf of Lyon. Just a few weeks before I arrived in July 2003, Montpellier Rugby Club was crowned champion of the second division, winning entry to the first division, or Top 16 as it was then.

A club's accession to the first division, once the hangover wears off, is typically followed by a mad scramble for more money to sign up players and boost squad depth and experience for the following season. The Ligue Nationale de Rugby lays down the dates for the official transfer season, which runs for about a month through June into July, during which time contracts are officially ratified. Most clubs will have started looking for players in January or February, and will have signed pre-contracts with most of their new recruits by May. So by the time the little club from the second division arrives, delighted to have earned the right to sit at the same table as the big boys, they realise that the big boys have already chomped through the best parts of what was on offer, and all that is left are scraps.

As chance would have it, I was one of those scraps. I had come to the end of my second contract with Perpignan, a town 100 miles further down the Mediterranean coast, just north of the Spanish border. Although a smaller town than Montpellier, Perpignan had a bigger club. This club had just made it into the final of the European Cup, and its ambition was to become part of the small circle of genuine heavyweights—Stade Français in Paris, Stade Toulousain in Toulouse, and, more recently, Biarritz Olympique in the Basque country on the Atlantic Coast—who have been consistently at the top of the pile in the French professional game. As a result, there had been an end-of-season clear-out of those players not considered up to scratch and, along with fourteen others of the 30-man squad, I had found myself out of a job.

This wasn't entirely unexpected, and through various agents I had been tarting myself around since late December —with decidedly mixed results. I had had one solid offer from Montferrand, but hoping for something better I had put them off and they had found someone else. I had really wanted to play for Stade Français in Paris, but a barrage of wheedling phone calls had met with nothing but silence. As far as the ten or so other clubs in the first division went, I felt like Goldilocks. The big ones were too big; after my experience with Stade Français I didn't bother trying Toulouse, who were in even less need of an aging journeyman. But the small ones, who were at least decent enough to appear interested, were too small.

Things were getting desperate—in fact they had been desperate for a while—when Montpellier, who looked as though they might be neither too big nor too small but just right, appeared on the scene. As far as the rugby went, I was well aware that Montpellier would struggle, but there are other things that you look for in a club. *Midi Olympique*, the French rugby weekly, had conducted a survey of players' preferred clubs, taking into account several quality-of-life factors as well as rugby. Montpellier had figured in a highly respectable fifth place, behind Toulouse, Biarritz, Paris and Perpignan, but in front of bigger names such as Castres, Clermont-Ferrand (Montferrand) and Bourgoin.

The day I was to sign in Montpellier, Biarritz, having just realised they were a lock short for the coming season, called to see if I were interested. After a few hours of indecision I decided I would be better off playing a relatively important role in Montpellier than sitting on the bench—or worse, as an afterthought—in the star-studded Biarritz team, and there was more chance of my girlfriend finding work in the economically dynamic town of Montpellier than the beach resort of Biarritz. On top of this, Montpellier were obviously keen to have me, and as already mentioned I am a sucker for flattery, although I have to admit I was disappointed that the ferocious bidding war for my services, for which I had been hoping, did not materialise.

The agent who would have signed me to Biarritz told me that I had made a mistake, and that we were going to spend a difficult year being steamrolled up front and torn apart out wide. It was with these comforting words ringing in my ears that on a sweltering July morning I rolled up to a ground borrowed from the local army barracks for the first day of training.

At Perpignan the first few weeks of pre-season training had taken place out of town on a borrowed ground, but the rest of the time we had trained at the stadium itself, or at the annexe next door. The stadium complex had also included the weights room, and, brilliantly, all our laundry had been done on site. Montpellier, I discovered, had more of a gypsy flavour. On any given day we might be at the stadium, or the military barracks, or just out of town at another borrowed field, or doing weights at any one of three different places. And if it rained all bets were off: you could be anywhere, or training might simply be cancelled. The strip worn for the game and the coloured bibs that we wore to distinguish ourselves at training were washed once a week, but after that we were on our own as far as laundry was concerned.

To be fair, Montpellier is a very young club, and by the time you read this a brand new state-of-the-art stadium with annexe grounds and wet-weather training pitches should be up and running. In any case, running around like blue-arsed flies trying to find the right ground does wonders in inducing humility, particularly in those of us who suffer from a hopeless sense of direction, as does dealing with the pile of reeking gear that has fermented in the kitbag you forgot to empty into the washing-machine.

Arriving in a new club is always difficult. For a start, there are all the obvious, non-rugby-related difficulties that revolve around moving to a new home. And then, as with any new job, you have to prove yourself to your new colleagues, while treading carefully through the potential bitchiness caused by your taking the place of someone who was part of the tight-knit community, and the widely held (and not entirely unfounded) suspicion that you are being paid more than the guys who got the team to where it is now.

French rugby is, of course, a small world, and if you're lucky you will already know some of the team, having played with them in another club. At Montpellier, there was at least one friendly face with whom I had played in Paris several years earlier. Unfortunately, there was also a senior player with whom I had an ongoing vendetta, having spent a winter afternoon a couple of seasons earlier trading cheap shots with him while we were wearing different jerseys.

As I tried to fit in, I spent some time worrying about the coming season. It was clear there was some genuine talent at Montpellier, but not nearly as much as there had been in Perpignan. This was logical, given Montpellier's late arrival and small budget: while it is not an absolute guarantee of success, money buys talent, pace and physical presence, so the smaller a club's cheque-book, the less it gets. To their credit, Montpellier had signed on for another two years nearly all the players who had played the season before, so that, having played their way into the first division, they would have the opportunity to show what they were worth. The club had then added a handful of experienced players who, like me, were coming to the end of their careers.

When I say 'to their credit', the club had acted honourably but not necessarily wisely: they could easily have jettisoned half a dozen players of limited potential, and signed the others for only one year, which would have been long enough to head-hunt replacements for those who hadn't adapted. Coming from a club like Perpignan, I was used to a culture of ambition that—in the spirit of the age of the mercenary—had little time for honourable gestures. While ruthless ambition can be short-sighted, there is something to be said for it when you are staring down the barrel of relegation.

The positive side of keeping on the same players is that the group clearly having the confidence of the club president is good for morale, and the social fabric is less likely to tear than if individuals were to try and pull in different directions, as often happens when things get difficult. Every club likes to think of itself as a family with tightly knit bonds, but in Montpellier this had been closer to reality than at most clubs. Players who had retired often stayed involved in some way, through coaching or in a less official role, and this made for a good atmosphere. You got the feeling the club looked after its own, and you were not simply a piece of meat to be junked when you passed your sell-by date. Understandably, this is increasingly rare in the professional world.

Obviously, though, a good atmosphere is no substitute for results. Two teams would go down to second division at the end of the year, and in the eyes of most pundits Montpellier was odds-on favourite to be one of them. To bridge the talent gap that existed between a good second-division side and the kind of team that could expect to be still in the first division at the end of the year, the coach decided to try bringing everyone up to scratch through drawn-out training sessions that in the summer heatwave seemed never-ending and often counterproductive: more quantity than quality. The team made progress, but I wasn't sure it would be enough.

The first few games of the year were friendlies, and not very encouraging. Luckily for us, 2003 was a World Cup year, so while the big teams' stars were battling for world supremacy in Australia, the rest of us played out an unimportant French cup competition, which allowed us to get to grips with the harsh realities of life in the first division without actually having the knife at our throats. The results were not promising—one win from six games—but not as bad as I had feared. The team took great pride in throwing everything into *le combat*, a good starting point but not really enough. It is possible to grind out a win simply through dogged defence and a good kicking game, but you have to be extremely good at both to pull it off on a regular basis. Top-level rugby is not really a choice between the rapier and the cudgel: *everyone* has a cudgel, so you better have one too, and the bigger the better. But you would be well-advised to have a rapier as well, and to know how to handle it.

We were happy enough smashing things up, but our swordsmanship wasn't what it might have been, so when we came to play our first championship game against the swashbuckling European Cup champions Toulouse it looked like we were on a hiding to nothing. They had several players unavailable on World Cup duty, but were still, on paper, vastly superior to us. Two minutes into the game they scored an effortless try from broken play and it looked as if all our worst fears were to be realised. Then something extraordinary happened. Stung by the prospect of being slaughtered in front of a home crowd, we clawed our way into the game, first getting an edge and then dominating outrageously. Toulouse scored a couple of catch-up tries at the end, but the final score had everyone—especially me—scratching our heads and rubbing our eyes: Montpellier 50, Toulouse 31.

Rugby is not the sort of game where upsets often occur, so this result was a big deal and gave us all a badly needed confidence boost. As it turned out it wasn't, though, the foretaste of a glorious run in the championship. After we scraped a win in the next home game, reality kicked in and we lost eight on the trot, slipping inexorably down the table towards the relegation zone, before getting our act together in the spring and finishing a quite satisfactory tenth in our first season in the Top 16. The next season was much the same. Widely seen as promising candidates for the drop, we had a good start with an extraordinary win early on against Stade Français, a big team, 49–26, but a worrying dip in the winter brought us dangerously close to going down, only to finish strongly in eleventh place.

The season we are facing will again be a difficult one for Montpellier: the Top 16 has been squeezed down to the Top 14, but two teams will still be relegated, so eleventh, which looked comfortable enough last year, will be stressful. The club has upped its budget to €6.6 million, from €5.5 million last year, and there is a little more talent around. As a result, as pre-season training starts everyone is feeling upbeat. At the training camp we agree that we should be aiming to finish the season between sixth and eighth in the championship.

From the outside this may sound unambitious. Surely, you may think, as professional sportsmen we should be aiming to win every game and thus the competition? A few years ago I would have agreed, but experience tells me that even banking on finishing in the top eight sounds like hubris. Montpellier is growing as a club, no doubt about it, but so are the other teams, and if you want to move up the ladder it means pushing someone off from higher up. Of the teams that finished in front of us last year there are perhaps two we could overtake—Brive and Narbonne—with the possibility of a third, Agen, should they have a bad year. That would have us in eighth place. To place higher than that would mean that one of the big clubs—the clubs qualified for the Heineken Cup, Europe's premier competition—would have to have a season way below par, or that we would have to have a blinder. Which isn't impossible, I suppose.

Equally, it's not impossible that we will have a shocker, be overtaken by the clubs behind us, and go down. But in all probability we will scrap our way through the season feeling threatened by the drop without it actually coming to that. In any case, that is as much as I dare hope for. In my last year in Paris when I was playing for Racing, the club went down and it makes for a hell of a season. Internal bickering, the threat of financial meltdown linked to the lack of results, and a general feeling of guilt at poor performance and your own inability to change the course of destiny are all things I would rather avoid, particularly as I think this will be my last year of rugby.

We start back on July 8, a week before we are supposed to according to the *convention collective* signed between the players' union and the clubs, but since we went on holiday at the start of June, a couple of weeks before everyone else, no one makes a fuss. Professional rugby in France runs on an eleven-month cycle (twelve if you are an international called up to play on the summer tours to the southern hemisphere), with competition finishing in June and starting again at the end of August after six weeks of pre-season over July and August.

Rugby is supposed to be a winter sport, but with 28 French Championship fixtures, nine European Cup fixtures, about a dozen international games, and a handful of friendlies at the start of the season, hardly a weekend goes by without a major game of some sort, and top players can play upwards of 40 games in a year. By comparison, players in other countries play a maximum of 30 or so games, international and domestic competitions combined. The jury is still out on the effect the French schedule has on the players' health, but in the meantime money is the motor: more competition equals more revenue from television and sponsors, and nothing looks like getting in the way of this equation. The players who play the most are generally the ones who get paid the most, so they tend not to argue.

Pre-season traditionally starts with a battery of physical tests and this year is no exception. Fat tests, speed tests, weight tests and fitness tests are all performed and statistics compiled with scientific rigour, and there is much discussion and excitement about various individual performances: the wingers are all over themselves to be the fastest man in the team, while the props do battle on the bench press. As I am consistently among the slowest, weakest and fattest it is not a moment I relish, although I am reassured by the knowledge that everyone forgets about the statistics as soon as we actually start playing rugby.

The year gets off to a particularly unimpressive start, even by my low standards, when I pull up lame halfway through the 12-minute test (running as far as possible round a track in 12 minutes—something I can normally do reasonably well). A bad knee that I have been carrying since last year's pre-season blows up, promising to hinder my preparation. If I were to be cynical about it I would call it a blessing in disguise, because the coach steadfastly refuses to see that we are overtraining, and at my advanced age I could well do without the first month of endless running and full-contact, mortal combat-style training sessions. At 33, I am the oldest player in the team.

The bad knee means that I have to do my fitness work on a winch, a sort of bicycle contraption for the upper body where you 'pedal' with your hands. As an engine of physical torture, it is right up there with a rowing ergometer, and it is with little regret that I rule myself out of doing even this with a spectacular, some might say virtuoso, display of incompetence, that has me slicing my hand open on the winch's revolving disc wheel when my sweaty palms slip off the handle. I narrowly miss cutting a tendon and am rewarded with total rest for two weeks, while everyone else slogs through the summer heat.

By the time I come back we are into the friendly games, just a couple of weeks out from the start of the championship. My injured knee is still playing up, so I tend to put most of my weight on my other knee, particularly when coming down to earth from line-out jumps. This is not a great idea—lifting in line-outs means you get up to heights that nature never intended, particularly when, like me, you weigh 110 kilograms and are not predisposed to feats of athleticism, so when you hit the ground you need both legs to properly brake your fall. Just before half-time against second-division Lyon, the inevitable happens when my supposedly good knee gives out, and although it doesn't hurt or even swell up there is an ominous clicking and scraping every time I use it.

This is a worry. If I was not unhappy about missing the grind of pre-season, I am less zen about missing the start of the season. I also have the unpleasant feeling that my body is starting to betray me. For years I have suspected that my mind was writing cheques that my body couldn't cash, and it may be that the metaphorical debt collector is now taking, if not a pound of flesh, at least a good handful of cartilage, and perhaps some other important tissue. Most of my generation have stopped playing, and I fear I may have signed up for one season too many and my body will let me down. This is compounded by the fact that, while I have considered myself an essential part of the starting line-up for the last two years, the club has had the foresight to bring in a new lock, an Englishman called Alex Codling, to beef up their options in the second row, and he will now have the chance to establish himself as number one while I am out of the running. I am all for healthy competition for starting jerseys within the team as long as I get mine.

There is even another young lock waiting in the wings, which makes six of us for three places (two on the field, one on the bench). This is too many for my liking, particularly as the others all look distressingly competent. Worse still, the young lock doesn't look as though he will be happy to bide his time waiting for his chance. He is Georgian, and although I say young this doesn't mean baby-faced. At 22 he is a great bear of a man, and seems to spend all his spare time in the weights room. His name is Mamuka Gorgodze and he is dubbed, inevitably, 'Gorgodzilla'—although if you value your life you don't say this to his face. During the pre-season mortal-combat sessions he ran around smashing people into the ground, both with ball in hand and with the kind of sledgehammer tackles that cave in ribcages.

One of his victims, our South African centre Rickus Lubbe —no lightweight himself at a respectable 102 kilograms— swore under his breath as he was picking himself up after being stomped by Gorgodzilla, and the beast quickly turned on him: 'What you say? You say I fuck my mother?' (His English isn't great, but he seems to have the basics under control.) It took the intervention of four of us to reassure him it was just an expression, the Gorgodze family honour was in no way being questioned, and no blood sacrifices would be necessary.

Luckily our other Georgian, Mamuka Magrikividledze, was on hand to help in the calming down. Although Mamuka is a good guy with a sense of humour, he is another 127-kilogram ogre who looks as if he eats babies for breakfast. God only knows what Georgian team runs look like. I imagine a horde of monsters tearing lumps of flesh out of each other, with the unforgiving Tbilisi winter as a backdrop.

My usual plan for dealing with enthusiastic, well-muscled youngsters who are looking hungrily at my jersey and show-ing off their physical prowess is to adopt a kind of Obi Wan Kenobi (Alec Guinness, not Ewan McGregor) aging-sage-who's-been-around-a-bit style of patter—something like, 'It's all very well standing there looking shiny and strong, there is much you have to learn before you can be ready.' In Gorgodzilla's case this is true: he so revels in his physical strength that he tends to disregard the rules of the game, and looks highly put out when referees have the cheek to penalise him for ripping people's arms off and beating them to death with the bloody limb, or whatever his circus trick of the moment happens to be.

Unfortunately we seem to have a communication problem —I'm talking but he's not listening. One day at scrum training we have too many locks and not enough loose forwards, and I take it upon myself to suggest it would be a good idea if he were to perhaps play in a different position. 'Mamuka, you play number eight.' He doesn't look happy about it, but complies for a few scrums before coming back to me, 'I have idea. *I* play lock, *you* play number eight.' The old Jedi mind trick, it seems, doesn't work on everyone.

From a layman's point of view, this talk of 127-kilogram behemoths sounds impressive. The terrifying thing for a spindly, six-foot-six, 110-kilogrammer like me is that these men are only just above average size. One of our props, a Samoan New Zealander called Philemon Toleafoa, tips the scales at 140 kilograms. This would be all very well if, as you would imagine, he lumbered around the park from scrum to line-out at the pace of an asthmatic snail, but instead he reaches alarmingly high speeds in a very short time, and takes great pleasure using his shoulder as a wrecking ball on any-one brave enough to be in his way. Our seven props average around 125 kilograms each, although there are a couple of lightweights of my weight. Before professional rugby came along and allowed players to spend more time in the gym, rugby players tended to be larger than average but only a few were genuinely outsize. These days you may get the impres-sion from watching a game on television, or even from seeing one live, that players are still of more or less ordinary size. This is misleading. Standing next to one another they look relatively normal, but alongside them average-sized people—about five-foot-eight and 70 kilograms—look like under-nourished leprechauns.

Home and Away

Our first championship game of the season is against Castres at home. Castres have always been a good side on paper, but for one reason or another they rarely make it into the semifinals. They are blessed with a sponsor, Pierre Fabre, who runs an eponymous pharmaceutical company that is big enough for him to write out large cheques to keep the club of this small town in the top half of the table.

This year they have brought in Laurent Seigne, formerly of Bourgoin and Brive, as coach. Seigne's methods are well-known in rugby circles for being a little old-fashioned. Gregor Townsend, the Scotland and British Lions first five-eighth, told me that, before one game at Brive, Seigne had made the forwards—boots and all—run over him and his fellow centre in the changing-room because he didn't consider them sufficiently enthusiastic about *le combat*. He also broke one player's nose with a head butt during a pre-match talk.

So it will be no surprise if Castres are more physical this year than they have been in the past. Some of them may be scarred for life, but then no one said it would be a cakewalk.

We have two locks out injured, so although I am not really ready to be playing I sit on the bench with both knees heavily strapped, praying that, if I get on, they will hold up. As we are running through warm-up exercises, Alex Codling, the English lock, vomits. He had warned me that this might happen because he suffers from some sort of lung disease, but the other boys don't know this and most of them don't look pleased, particularly because he throws up in the middle of a grid in which we are about to start doing forward rolls. To top off the performance he then moves slightly to his right so someone else has to roll forward into what is left of his lunch. Most of us shuffle a couple of feet away from the ugly little pile while trying to stay focussed, and someone who hasn't seen what's happened arrives to take his place.

Castres have a powerful forward pack based around Kees Meeuws, the former All Black tighthead prop. We hold up all right up front, but start to get pinged by the referee for things that are more the result of inexperience than being over-powered. There are plenty of errors on both sides; it's still early in the season, summer really, and crushingly hot, so the ball is slippery with sweat and neither team manages much continuity. We seem to grind away without much reward, while they get easy penalties from scrums, which their full-back, the robotic Romain Teulet, kicks with dispiriting regularity. We manage a couple of three-pointers ourselves, and when the half-time whistle blows at 12–6 to them I have a feeling that we are in with a chance if we can just get some forward momentum.

The first quarter of an hour of the second half shows up my misplaced optimism for the wishful thinking it is. Their forwards are the ones who get the forward momentum going. Two quick tries, and with 25 minutes to go the game is more or less over at 24–6. I am sent on to take Alex Codling's place just after the second try, and after we kick a penalty I allow myself to think that perhaps the cavalry has arrived in the nick of time. (Reserves love believing this kind of crap.) But really I do absolutely nothing to stem the tide. I get side-stepped by their centre, and by the time my wobbly knees react and get me back to where I need to be to make the tackle he is already five yards past me. A few minutes later I am one of three people holding up Meeuws when he scores. In fact, my only satisfaction comes from landing a good punch on their replacement hooker after the little bastard bites me in a maul. With about ten minutes to go we score a consolation try. It makes the score look a little less ugly, but 34–16 is still a kick in the teeth, and a very bad start to the season.

At the after-match we see television replays showing that Meeuws didn't actually ground the ball, but by then it's too late: the use of the television referee is only for games that are televised live, and Canal+ rarely screens our games. So the post-mortem clutching at straws starts. Our new fly-half, former French international David Aucagne, although he had played well and kicked goals as required, had managed to butcher the easiest of chances after chipping through a kick that was missed by their cover defence, knocking the ball on when all he had to do was pick it up and fall over the line under the posts.

To try and cheer ourselves up, we play the game of re-calculating the scores according to what might have been. Subtract Meeuws' try and the conversion from their total, add on Aucagne's 'try' and the imaginary conversion to ours, and abracadabra, it was a close-run thing at 27–23. From here it is only a short step to questioning a couple of refer-eeing decisions that gave them kickable penalties and—*voila!*—23–21 to us would have been the final score had the game been played in a truly just universe. This is the kind of wilful self-delusion that did for Madame Bovary.

From a completely objective viewpoint, 34–16 is probably a fair reflection of the gap between the two teams, and therefore not much of a drama. Castres look like a good side and should beat plenty of other teams. The problem is that we are playing in France, and when you play at home in France there is no room for objectivity. Here, rugby is more of an art than a science. Despite all the video analysis and number-crunching of the modern game, part of its charm is that it remains bloody-mindedly irrational. I have already mentioned the French idea of *l'esprit de clocher*—the credo of collective duty to the town, the team and the jersey. The peculiarity of the French version of 'pride in the jersey' is that it manifests itself much more strongly when you play at home. At home, the team is like the local militia, entrusted with the sacred duty of repelling the invaders and upholding the honour of the town—and everyone is watching. It doesn't matter that, intellectually, the players are capable of seeing the absurdity of playing differently at home and away. Everyone recognises that the pitch is the same size, the number of players the same for both sides, the ball the same shape, the referee (arguably, but we'll come back to that) neutral. *You win home games.* Away games you try to win, but at the back of your mind there is always the thought that if you lose, well, there's always next week, and next week is at home.

This highly developed sense of geographical awareness is linked to another very French idea, that of *terroir*, the notion that a product draws its identity from the soil in which it is produced and its character from the culture that surrounds it. I can't help but find this romantic sense of rootedness appealing. Rugby thrives in the hothouse environment of small French towns. Apart from the fully fledged cities of Paris and Toulouse, and to a lesser extent Montpellier and Mont-ferrand, all the clubs in the Top 14 are based in towns that have populations of a 100,000 or less. The team's performance is a measure of the town's virility and skill, and gives its citizens an opportunity for civic pride when they compare their status with that of their big city cousins. Living in this kind of emotional climate, the players feel obliged to respond to expectations, because as their town's champions their honour is on the line more than anyone's.

In spite of the arrival of the professional era and the widespread use of mercenaries like me, to whom it had never previously occurred that you might play differently on one rugby ground as opposed to another, expectations remain the same. Yet even the French players are from somewhere else originally—most clubs have no more than a handful of genuine home-grown players—and it seems odd that, say, a Catalan playing for Biarritz or a Basque playing for Bourgoin should feel any greater surge of emotional power playing 'at home'' than would an Australian, but it is still the case.

The home club does have a few very slight advantages. The home changing-room is normally slightly bigger and better equipped; the players know the ground better and can read swirling wind conditions; the home club always provides the match ball, and some clubs have different makes of ball that kickers find fly differently. Here in Montpellier (and I suspect everyone else is the same), the ball boys are told to swiftly gather balls that we kick into touch, so the opposition can't take quick throw-ins.

Most importantly there is the crowd, which likes to think of itself as the sixteenth man, capable of influencing a match with its voice. At Perpignan we used to let the other team run out first, leave them out there soaking up the whistles and the jeers for a minute or so, and then arrive to a roar that made the hairs stand up on the back of my neck. These days the teams have to come out of the tunnel at the same time, and the ground announcer is obliged to read out a little speech exhorting the fans to encourage their team in a spirit of fair play—for what that's worth. The opposition kicker, their fullback under a high ball, a referee or touch judge making a questionable decision (and generally speaking, any decision that goes against the home team is considered question-able)—everyone gets a raspberry.

And it is quite possible that the actors on the field, both players and officials, are influenced by this, consciously or not. More than once I have seen passes that were not forward whistled by referees, simply because the crowd called for it. But even this hardly accounts for the difference—usually about 20 points, depending on the exact circumstances— between a team's performance at home and away.

It had never used to make much difference to me where I played, whether there was a big crowd and, if there was, whether they were for me or against me. I suppose that, like anyone, my ego is puffed up by the presence of a lot of spectators. And even if the crowd were screaming insults, at least it meant they were paying attention. But this didn't affect the way I played. As with most New Zealanders, my motivation was internal, or at most revolved around what my teammates might think of me if I performed badly.

But I am conscious of having undergone a change in the way I feel during my time in France. Where I was once calm and phlegmatic (which the French see as typically Anglo-Saxon), I now get wound up just watching a game I think is important, and can blow up for the mildest of reasons. It is impossible to live in a vacuum, and the culture in which I operate has rubbed off on me. When I play a home game there is urgency to my preparation, but when playing away I am quite relaxed. I don't think this affects my performance, but I may be kidding myself. In any case, the stress of losing a game that you know you need to win is so great that, given Montpellier's away record, I would give myself an ulcer if I worried equally about every game. Over the last two seasons combined we have won only two championship games away from home.

Perhaps the best known example of the home-and-away mindset is the 1999 World Cup semifinal between France and New Zealand. As part of their preparation, the French team had visited New Zealand a few months before the competition, and been annihilated by 50 points. They had been particularly depressed by this result because they hadn't thought they had played badly: they had simply been beaten by a vastly superior team.

The semifinal was to be played at Twickenham, in front of a crowd of largely English spectators, with a smattering from New Zealand and France. The English spectators were supposedly neutral, although the French always assume that English-speakers invariably stick together: '*Vous êtes tous des Breteesh.*' But the French arrived in the role of underdog, and an All Black victory seemed so inevitable that the *Breteesh* decided to cheer for their European neighbours. It would be simplistic to say that this alone led to the extraordinary upset that followed. The All Blacks, it seemed, had peaked too early in their preparation and appeared tactically naïve, while the French, after a dismal start, grew progressively stronger, helped by the serendipitous arrival, through injury, of certain key players originally omitted from selection. But the psychological impact that hearing '*Allez les Bleus!*' ring around fortress Twickenham had on the French players was immense, and played an important role in their famous victory.

So this loss to Castres is discouraging for several reasons. Losing this heavily at home means we are clearly not competitive with the big boys, which is bad news because our next three games are all against teams who are qualified for Europe, and our next home game is against Toulouse, who, unfortunately for us, don't seem to suffer from the French version of travel sickness. Their supporters' chant on away trips is '*On vient, on gagne, et on s'en va,*' an irritating Gallic version of '*Veni, vidi, vici*'. It is quite possible that, after four rounds of the competition, we will resemble one of the more disappointing entrants in the Eurovision Song Contest: *Montpellier, nul points.*

This, in turn, will mark us out as a potentially winnable away game in the eyes of all the other teams, so they will approach the match in a different way than they might otherwise have done. Vultures. The first ten games of the Top 14 are to be played back-to-back this year, so if we start off on a losing streak we won't have the opportunity to gather our breath for some time. From a personal viewpoint, I had been hopeful that with a bit of adrenalin my knees would miraculously rise to the occasion, even though I was having trouble running in a straight line, but they remain resolutely uncooperative. I will need to stop playing for at least two weeks and hope they come right with physiotherapy.

The good news is that most of the teams that we are counting on being between us and the bottom of the table have suffered the same fate we have. Toulon, who have just arrived from the second division, went down to Biarritz, while Pau and Bayonne lost to Montferrand and Toulouse respectively. No one scores a bonus point (achieved by scoring four tries, or being defeated by seven points or less).

Narbonne, who I hoped would get off to an equally bad start, have somehow managed to beat Stade Français, and Brive have beaten Bourgoin. These last two games at least hold to home-and-away form: neither Narbonne nor Brive would have a hope of winning in Paris or Bourgoin. The fact that four teams have lost at home is ominous for the future of the championship. It looks as though we will quickly be divided into 'haves' and 'have-nots'.

From a mercenary point of view, winning and losing is a more complex equation than it may look at face value. If you are in the starting line-up, then obviously you want to win. Being in a winning team is always more fun, whether you are amateur or professional. There may also be win bonuses, though they are rare in French rugby and I believe rightly so: if you have got this far it is because you are a natural competitor and love playing the game, so while you will choose a club largely according to the size of the monthly cheque, when you are actually on the field you have a one-track mind, and promises of more cash are unnecessary.

Things get complicated when you remember that a team is made up from a squad of more than 30 players, of whom only 15 can be on the field at any one time. It's one thing if you are injured, or a young player with a future who needs to develop his skills in the second team and have occasional run-outs in less important games. But once you have arrived at a certain age, and you are not injured or being rested, the fact you are watching a game rather than playing it is hard to swallow.

Some players resolutely accept the coach's decision to put them on the bench or drop them completely, but I am not one of them, and I am sure I am not the only player to have sat in the stands watching someone else play in what I consider to be my jersey, and to hope that the team loses and the coach realises the error of his ways and reinstates me the following week.

Unfortunately, this is something of a luxury. If you are locked in a life-or-death relegation battle, as seems to be the case with Montpellier all the time, you know that losing a must-win game can lead to trouble. Relegation can lead to unemployment at worst, and at best a drop in your market value as a player and a subsequent scramble to find a new club. So the ideal solution is that the team wins but that the guy playing in my position has a nightmare of a game, bringing me back into the frame without the team having to suffer for my egotism. Like many players I am slightly superstitious, so I don't stoop to hoping for an expedient injury as I suspect that would be bad karma. And filling in for someone because they're injured feels a little like keeping the seat warm.

The Saturday after the Castres game, we travel away to Clermont-Ferrand. My knees rule me out of playing, so what I know of the game is from the subsequent video analysis and different reports. Montferrand are a strange club in that they always have a pile of money. Their budget, at €10.6 million, is second only to Toulouse, and is largely provided by the Michelin family, who run the world-famous tyre company out of this industrial city in the heart of the Massif Centrale. This means the team have a pleiad of French and international stars and are consistently thought of as potential

French champions, and yet, despite participating at élite level since 1925 and making it to the final on seven separate occasions, they have never won a championship.

Last year they had a disastrous start to the season, which saw them at the bottom of the table halfway through, before they sacked their coach and brought in Olivier Saïsset, my old coach from Perpignan. They went on to win a remarkable series of games and just qualify for the European Cup. They are not a team that inspires fear, but they are full of potential and could run riot at any moment if you give them the sniff of a chance. The previous weekend they beat Pau at Pau quite comfortably so are on the crest of a wave, while we know our chances of a win are slim to nothing. Still, we have to improve on the outing against Castres, so we throw everything into it.

The game is a tit-for-tat affair, with each team having their moments. Our line-out causes them trouble, robbing them of munitions with which they might overrun us, and we give them quite a run for their money, even leading 15–17 at one point in the second half, before cracking defensively in the last half-hour. Coco Aucagne kicks a penalty just before the end, which brings us up to a respectable 29–23. So we end up with the bonus point for defence, which has everyone reasonably happy as we open our account to get us off the floor of the championship table.

Fear and Loathing

Toulouse are again the reigning European champions, and by anyone's standards they are a good side. They arrive in Montpellier missing Fabien Pelous, the French lock and captain, and Isitolo Maka, the ex-All Black number eight, but their line-up remains mouth-watering for the aficionado and cold-sweat-inducing for the opposition. Individuals such as Welsh captain Gareth Thomas, Yannick Jauzion and Fred Michalak ooze class, and most of the players on the bench would walk into any other side

Like Montferrand, the team is full of highly paid stars, but that is where the two clubs part company. These men mesh together in a side that understands the culture of winning. Under coach Guy Novès, who has been in place for ten years, Toulouse have been so successful that, by their own high standards, any year they are not European or French champion is a bad year. It helps that they have the biggest budget in the championship—€17.15 million—and that the city of Toulouse is the acknowledged capital of French rugby so they have a rich pool of talent on which to draw. The mercurial genius of Michalak, for example, was discovered more or less by accident, when he was thrown into the first team at the tender age of 18 after a string of injuries to the Toulouse halfbacks.

We are up against it and we know it.

Once again, my knees have me watching from the sideline, and within ten minutes I am trying to avert my eyes and think happy thoughts as what is happening on the field looks like turning into a massacre. Toulouse are already 10–0 up. However, we dig in and batter away at their forwards. The Toulouse pack are no pushover, but they are not as likely to leave you floundering in their wake as are their backs, so you are better off trying to take them on up front, rather than sending the ball wide, or kicking deep, and exposing yourself to counterattacks.

Gaining ground by centimetres, we start putting them under pressure and go to the break 6–13, although with our big Samoan centre, Ali Koko, getting a yellow card for a high tackle just before half-time, we can look forward to an uphill grind. We kick another penalty shortly after the break, and at 9–13 are still in the game with ten minutes to go. However, we have been harshly penalised a couple of times in the line-out by the referee, Monsieur Mené, and the platform for our driving mauls is weakened when we need it most. (Mené whistles us for fake jumps, but two weeks later will let exactly the same thing go when refereeing a 'big' team.) In the last ten minutes we crack, and when Toulouse score two penalties and a try to Thomas, we can muster only a penalty at the death: 12–24. No bonus point, *nada*.

The following week, we are up against Bourgoin. Bourgoin are a solid team, based around an excellent forward pack with French internationals Pascal Papé, Olivier Milloud and Julien Bonnaire, and an efficient kicking game from Benjamin Boyet at fly-half and Alexander Peclier at fullback. They haven't lost at home in the championship for something like three years, and let's face it, Montpellier are unlikely to break that run.

Club Sportif Bourgoin-Jallieu, to give it its full name, resides in an agglomeration of two small towns just outside Lyon, in the shadow of the alps, remarkable for nothing much other than the consistent success of their rugby club. Trivia fans may be intrigued to know that their colours, sky-blue and claret, are copied from the Birmingham football club Aston Villa: apparently the club was founded by an English expatriate. Its money comes mainly from its president, Pierre Martinet, a catering tycoon.

Although Bourgoin have been European-qualified for some time, their small squad of only 28 professionals means they are never really competitive in the Heineken Cup. In 2005 they suffered a 90-point thrashing in Dublin against Leinster, and are unlikely to ever threaten the big three. Their depressed local economy and rickety stadium hint at an uncertain future. Their home-grown players, their strength for so long, are being slowly picked up by the bigger clubs with bigger salaries.

For the moment, though, they are a damn sight bigger than we are, so it is with some satisfaction that we give them a fright, leading 3–0 for half an hour, before they score a converted try. At half-time it is 7–3 and unfortunately our young centre, Seb Mercier, thrown in at the deep end because of injury, misjudges a pass a couple of metres out when he could have just slid into the line. A try would have made the second half more interesting; instead they canter out to a comfortable 17–3 win.

A month later Bourgoin host Agen, and the aging Stade Pierre Rajon is the scene of one of French rugby's famous *bagarres générales*, or all-in brawls. After the half-time whistle blows, Luc Lafforgue, the Agen captain, goes over to the Bourgoin halfback Michael Forrest, says something, then clocks him. Predictably, all hell breaks loose. Most of the players were on their way to the changing-room but they turn around and start laying into their opposite numbers—or, failing that, anyone within reach. Spectators lean over the railings to get in their tuppence worth, the referee blows his whistle to no effect, and the rain of kicks and punches continues to fall on all sides for the best part of a minute, as scores, real or imagined, are settled.

Eventually things calm down and, as is often the case in a whirlwind of enthusiastically thrown but poorly aimed punches, no one is seriously hurt. The referee hands out red cards to the two captains, Lafforgue and Bonnaire, and everyone goes off to the changing shed for ten minutes to rediscover their *sang-froid*. Bourgoin have their stadium suspended for a game and so have to play a match away from home, and the two captains are suspended for two months but let off with less for good behaviour. As the match was televised, the punch-up is quickly taken up by various television channels and re-broadcast, occasionally with hand-wringingly pious commentary about how scandalous and shocking we should find the violence. However, the action is gleefully devoured by most of the viewing public, particularly rugby fans, who have never minded a few uppercuts to go with their up-and-unders.

Rugby players are often referred to as modern gladiators. Ice hockey, American Football and Australian Rules are the only other team sports that can be said to approach the same physical intensity, and in all of them the occasional dust-up is considered part and parcel of the game. If we're honest, it is also part of the attraction, because people love watching a scrap. From schoolyard to bar-room, the one thing certain to draw a good crowd is the shout of 'Fight! Fight!'

Even if you stay within the rules, with the move toward the high-impact game the physical confrontation is still spectacularly dangerous. People used to love watching Jonah Lomu running with the ball, not just because he had exceptional grace and agility but also because there was a genuine whiff of danger if anyone tried to stop him. This may not have registered with the casual observer, but as a rugby player who is pleased never to have been in a position to have had to try to tackle Lomu myself, I feel nothing but admiration for the players (most of them much smaller than me) who were in front of him, and at least made an effort. They must have felt they were taking their life in their hands, and were probably only a slightly misjudged tackle away from that being the case. Such action may look balletic and aesthetically pleasing to the people clapping politely in the stands, or watching slow-motion replays from the comfort of their sofas. On the field, though, it is nature red in tooth and claw. Rugby is a respectable version of blood sport.

Because there is always an element of danger, there is, naturally, fear. In order to overcome this, players often use anger, supposedly channelling the adrenalin into a useful and more controllable energy. This is what getting 'fired up' is all about, although most players would be hard-pressed to admit it because physical fear is seen as cowardice, and no one wants to be thought of as suffering from that. And many players are not conscious of fear as such. I didn't feel it until I was relatively old, and had seen players suffer serious injuries.

Using anger, and even hate, as tools is, however, emotionally lazy and, particularly for hot-blooded Latin types, adds to the danger. (Anglo-Saxons tend to keep their motivation inside a disciplined framework.) The game demands a certain amount of precision and constant decision-making, and over 80 minutes anger, although useful in short, intense bursts, is counterproductive. I have seen players crying with emotion before going on to the pitch because they were so wound up, and this is not helpful. If, for example, you're a hooker, you have to throw the ball into a line-out at exactly the right height and speed to make sure your side win it— wanting to rip out the opposition's throats is no use at all. Still, anger is commonly employed in France, where it is often confused with courage, particularly by smaller teams who know they are going to struggle on talent alone and are looking for something to compensate.

French rugby has more frequent boil-overs than rugby elsewhere. The stories I have heard about the sport in 'the old days'—only about 20 or 30 years ago—are enough to make your hair curl, even when taken with the obligatory grain of salt. Various individuals have regaled me with tales of what can only be described as psychopathic behaviour: taking 10-metre run-ups to boot people in the head, crippling players by wrenching joints into unnatural angles, and so on. One club allegedly turned out the lights in the corridor just as the two teams were lining up together to go on to the field, thereby offering their boys the chance of a surprise attack on the opposition under the cover of darkness and out of the referee's line of sight. The opportunity, I was told, was not wasted.

Toulon, only slightly more subtle, used to deliberately send the kick-off directly into touch at the start of their home games, so they could start with a scrum on the halfway line, followed by an inevitable flurry of fists that allowed them to remind the opposition of the importance of following the script—that is, we are playing at home so we are going to win, and if you want to get in the way of that you will see hell unleashed, and this is just a taste. Such tales are told with misty eyes and big grins. These days, thankfully, the use of the yellow card system, or 'sin-bin', has made a big difference. Referees hesitate to send a player off for the whole game for a single measly punch, particularly when it could be justified retaliation for an unseen misdemeanour, but they have fewer qualms about sending guys off for ten minutes. Everyone knows that being a man down for ten minutes can turn a close game, so players are not as quick on the draw as they used to be.

To outsiders the violence is shocking. I remember walking behind two officials from the Irish province Connacht after an unimportant European Shield game last season. We had lost by 50 points the week before in Ireland, and then scraped out a slim victory in the home game, more by foul means than fair, and there had been a number of unpleasant incidents. One of the Irishmen was saying to the other how disgusted their boys were, and the other replied, 'It's just not rugby.' Feeling slightly shamefaced, I mentioned this to my fellow lock Michel Macurdy, who, unabashed, replied, 'They shouldn't have put 50 points on us.'

In France, I'm afraid it *is* rugby. But it is so engrained in the culture that the French don't think of it as unusual. During a game against Australia in 2005, Fabien Pelous, the French captain, elbowed Brendan Cannon in the face, causing an injury that obliged the Australian hooker to leave the field and have several stitches put in so he could continue. Pelous did this in open play, out in the middle of the field, but so far away from the ball that the referee and touch judges didn't notice.

After the game, when the Australians were understandably upset, he said they needed to wait and see what the video replay looked like, obviously hoping the incident had not been picked up by the cameras. Unfortunately for him it had been, and the images were appalling. When asked to justify his action, he couldn't even say it was retaliation for some unseen skulduggery on Cannon's part, just that Cannon had been in the way and deliberately blocking him.

I have a lot of respect for Pelous as a player, and I have done some dumb things in the heat of action on the rugby field so I'm not going to throw stones. What was shocking, though, was that Bernard Laporte, the French coach, berated the French media, saying they shouldn't have shown the images and be making such a fuss. He went on to say this would never have happened in New Zealand. That is simply not true, as witness the 'spear tackle' by the All Black captain, Tana Umaga, on Brian O'Driscoll during the 2005 Lions tour: although judged an over-vigorous clearing-out by the disciplinary board, it led news stories for the best part of a week.

Having said that, there is much hypocrisy about the use of violence on the rugby field. In his book *A Year in the Centre*, O'Driscoll complained about being eye-gouged while playing against Argentina. 'Don't ask me why they do it. It has no place in rugby. The best way to put a cheat in his place is by consistently beating him.' This sounds fair enough, until you read the Welsh centre Gavin Henson complaining in his book *My Grand Slam Year* that he had been eye-gouged by O'Driscoll, who apparently rubbed it in by asking, 'How do you like that, you cocky little fucker?'

When I arrived in France in 1997 I was shocked by the violence. At 25 I wasn't old, but I wasn't exactly wet behind the ears either. However, the first game I played—a run-out with the Bs in Dijon while I waited for my licence to come through—so opened my eyes that my initial reaction was to close them again as quickly as possible, before someone stuck their fingers in them. I should have realised there was something unusual going on when I saw some of my new team-mates putting on what looked like cricket boxes. Why the hell would anyone need to protect their balls in a rugby game?

Mercifully, no one assaulted my unsuspecting genitalia, but my nose was broken by a punch at the first line-out, and the game resembled a street fight. At one point a line-out degenerated into a brawl on one side of the field, but the ball made its way out to the opposite wing where the backs had their own little disagreement to sort out. On both sides of the field, players and spectators were getting stuck in with boots and fists, and even umbrellas and gumboots, while Dijon's resident New Zealander and I were left standing in the middle of the pitch, not knowing whether to laugh, cry or start punching each other.

A bit of niggle is an occupational hazard for rugby players, especially forwards, all over the world. The contact area, particularly in rucks and mauls, is a pile-up of bodies, every one of whom is intent on extracting maximum advantage to his side from the effort he puts in—whether getting the ball back for his team, pinching it from the opposition, or simply getting in the way of the other lot. The law has a number of grey areas that can be exploited, and even the best referees have trouble keeping track of what all 30 players are doing at any one time.

Everyone has their own way of dealing with this, but people who are bending the rules should not be surprised to receive a little discouragement from the opposition who see the hand reaching into the ruck or feel the pull on the jersey from behind. Rugby players pride themselves on being hard men, but the difference between what it means to be 'hard'— respected for your ruthless, uncompromising attitude that inspires respect, if not fear, in the opposition—and 'dirty'— over the top—is a knife edge. Violence is only indiscipline if you get caught. Otherwise, physical intimidation is seen as a useful weapon.

My club coach at Marist St Pats in Wellington, Kevin Horan, a hard man from whom I learned a lot, used to tell us, 'Take the smack in the mouth, put your hands in your pockets and take the three points.' This epitomised what I think of as the right attitude to violence: shit happens, but always keep in mind the greater good of the team. It's about self-sacrifice, putting your body on the line, and not getting involved in vendettas that will distract you from the job. It is high-minded and I used to live by it. The problem is that it has one huge blind spot: it assumes the referee will spot the bastard who's had a go at you and take appropriate action.

One of the great specialties of French rugby is *la four-chette*, the eye-gouge. This is particularly effective because it is discreet. In the kind of car-crash situation that is the ruck or maul, with bodies arriving from all directions, it is very difficult for an observer to see a finger slipping unobtrusively into someone's eye. But you, the owner of the eye, know all about it, and quickly forget about whatever you are doing. The only thing that matters is getting that bloody finger out of there. You try to hold on to the finger so that you can see who the owner is, but invariably it slips back into the grunting morass that surrounds you.

It is a particularly unpleasant feeling having a dirty fingernail scraping along the back wall of your eye socket. It's even worse if, like me, you wear contact lenses and then have to fiddle around trying to get the lens back in place, or grope around on the ground looking for the tiny transparent object, without which the rest of the game is going to be hard to follow. In fifteen years of rugby in New Zealand I was eye-gouged twice, and I remember feeling physically sick afterwards that anyone would stoop so low. Within the first month of being in France I lost count of the number of times it happened.

I should now own up to having been in the wrong in a couple of eye-gouging incidents myself. In a court of law, the defence would plead extenuating circumstances: in both cases we were playing 'must win' matches at home in Montpellier that really were 'must win': defeat would mean we had one foot—or more—in the second division. These games are referred to as 'life or death', which with hindsight sounds overblown, but it is easy to lose perspective. And in both cases my victims were serial offenders. After a three-match losing streak we were just ahead of Biarritz, but couldn't score from our usually successful five-metre line-out drives. There were probably any number of reasons for this, including our own incompetence, but at the time the most glaring seemed to be the Biarritz hooker, Jean-Michel Gonzalez, bush-pigging his way into the middle of our maul and then somehow pulling it down cleverly enough to avoid being penalised.

After he had done this for the third time, I decided someone needed to discourage him. I opted for my first foray into one of the great French traditions and stuck my finger in his eye. Since it was my first time I was a bit nervous, and not wanting to do any serious damage, and a bit worried about the icky feeling of shoving a digit into another man's skull cavity, I didn't push hard enough. But I had another crack and it went in, and he looked gratifyingly unhappy. We were both face-to-face on the floor, so he knew very well who had done it. At the after-match we had a beer and I apologised. He replied with a smile, '*C'est le jeu, c'est le jeu*'—'That's the way the game is played.' He is of the old, old school, and having played in the first division for nearly twenty years and been capped for France thirty-four times it wasn't anything he hadn't seen at least a hundred times before.

We lost that game, but it is worth pointing out that the following year we played Biarritz in similar circumstances and towards the end of the game had a chance for a line-out drive from a penalty about 15 metres out—and again Gonzo came around on the wrong side of the maul, but this time with his head up, more for form's sake than with any real determination, which meant the referee could see him; he was even laughing as he did it. We duly got another penalty, pushed over from five yards out and won. I would probably be flattering myself to say that his treatment the previous year had changed his attitude, but you never know.

The second time around we were playing neighbouring Béziers in a derby match, and a three-match losing streak had blown out to a very worrying seven-match losing streak.

Bézier's hooker, Sebastian Bruno, had been mentioned in our team talk as having been particularly effective at slowing down our ball in the rucks in the away game that we had narrowly lost, and it was imperative he not do it again.

In my experience, no one actually singles out a member of the opposition and says, 'We have to get so-and-so off the park.' This would be considered ethically dodgy. However, there is an open-ended nature to certain instructions that allows for plausible deniability, while indicating that our best interests would be met were so-and-so less intimately involved with proceedings than he might have been planning. Of course, these instructions can be interpreted in any number of ways.

Anyway, Bruno was up to his old tricks again almost immediately, and I found myself with my finger in his eye suggesting that he would spend a more pleasant evening were he to remain out of our rucks. I don't know whether it made any difference, but we squeaked home and stayed up.

The other trick, just as effective as the eye-gouge but without the uncomfortable guilty feeling that (in my case at least) goes with it, is simply putting your hand near the eyes of the guy who has his hands on the ball or on the wrong side of the ruck. Everyone knows that this is the prelude to the dirty finger going in, so there is a rising feeling of panic in the victim, who immediately takes evasive action.

Obviously, eye-gouging is illegal and I am in no way condoning it. More than one player has partially lost their sight because of it, and being responsible for depriving anyone of their sight is not something anyone in their right mind would want to have on their conscience. I'm telling you about it simply because it happens. And one of the reasons it happens is because it seems to be widely accepted. The French Fédération has a recommended six-month suspension period for anyone caught eye-gouging, but it is almost impossible to catch the perpetrators.

In my first year in France I played for Racing against Montauban in Montauban, and ended up on the wrong side of a ruck trying to pilfer a ball. One of the opposition eye-gouged me, right in front of the referee, who duly blew his whistle and awarded a penalty against the owner of the offending digit. A penalty—the same punishment that is meted out to players who are offside, or backs who creep up inside the ten-yard zone before a line-out is deemed to be over. Not a red card followed by a six-month suspension. Only one player has been suspended for eye-gouging since I have been playing in France, Richard Nones from Colomiers, and he was suspended not by the French but by the European disciplinary board in 1998. He appealed on the grounds that he was innocent and that the touch judge who cited him was mistaken. There was a lot of French huffiness, largely because it was considered ludicrous to suspend anyone from their job for two years for such a banal crime.

The attitude of French referees tends to be more *laissez-faire* than that of their British and Commonwealth counterparts. This is not necessarily the fault of the ruling body, which has laid down reasonably strict guidelines in an effort to discourage violence. Rather, the men in the middle who have to enforce the laws often don't have the heart to do so.

The French attitude is perhaps best summed up in the language. A player who goes round smacking the opposition because they've been cheating is known as *le justicier*, the bringer of justice who casts himself in the role of judge, jury and executioner. There doesn't seem to be any irony involved. (Tellingly, the 'Anglo-Saxon' style of abiding by the law in the spirit of good sportsmanship is known as *le fairplay*—a word that has had to be imported because there isn't a French equivalent.)

One year it was announced that there was to be a crackdown on retaliation. The man who started a fracas was to be issued a yellow card, but the *justicier* who tried to finish it was to see red. Shortly after this we played a home game in which one of our players was kicked by one of the opposition's. As I was standing next to the man with the frisky boots, I felt honour-bound to have a slap at him. The referee saw the whole thing and called us both over. Both teams had been reminded of the new ruling and I was getting ready to be first into the showers as he went for his pocket. Out came a yellow for the other guy. The referee turned to me. 'You shouldn't have punched him,' he said. Then he sighed and shrugged, 'But it was a reflex action, and I understand. But you must not do it again!' I can't help sympathising with the referee in this kind of situation: the thinking behind the law is fine in theory, but in practice you couldn't really apply it without encouraging mayhem. If it had been enforced, coaches up and down the land would have been encouraging their troops along the lines of, 'Get your retaliation in first then, lads.'

History, Culture and Cash

I t's the fifth game of the season and already we have the knife at our throat. With a grand total of one point from the four previous outings, we are equal second to last with Toulon, one point ahead of Pau. Bayonne have seven points, comfortably ahead of us, after a home win against Pau and an away draw at Brive. If we lose today we are in all sorts of trouble, because Bayonne, unlike Castres and Toulouse, are a little team, and if we can't beat the little teams when we play at home then we simply aren't up to it.

Bayonne resemble us in many ways, with a forward-oriented game that they seem to have trouble exporting from their home ground. They arrived in the first division last year and did well to stay up, and now they are looking to con-solidate and move away from the danger zone at the bottom of the table. They are a much older club, formed by a group of rowers (officially they are part of an omnisport club known as *l'Aviron Bayonnais*—Bayonne Rowing) who were looking for an energetic winter sport a hundred years ago and who won their first French championship in 1913. Montpellier Rugby Club, a youngster by comparison, is celebrating its twentieth birthday in 2006. Bayonne are direct rivals with us for relegation.

Once again I am on the bench, and I go on after only quarter of an hour when Michel Macurdy breaks his hand. My knees are still heavily strapped—this is my first game back—but, mercifully, they seem to be doing more or less as they are told. We are already 7–0 up and quickly pull out to 10–0. With ten minutes to go to half-time their back-rower Yannick Lamour gets a yellow card, but even with one man up we can't capitalise when we should and are in danger of getting the shakes. All it would need is a quick try to put Bayonne back in the game and we could all start snarling at each other in typically French fashion over whose fault it is and the whole thing could fall apart.

I don't recall ever playing in an non-French team that did anything other than encourage each other on the field, though my memory may be selectively glossing over the darker moments. But, under pressure, French rugby players have the nasty habit of stating the obvious. There is nothing more irritating on a rugby field than having your team-mates tell you that you are screwing up, especially when you are well aware of this. While playing for Perpignan I missed a tackle that led to a try, and my captain said to me, 'You had to tackle him. Why didn't you tackle him? They scored a try because of your missed tackle.'

Different people deal with this in different ways. Some

blow it up into a full-scale argument, while others stalk off in a sulk. It's difficult to take it on the chin. You're thinking, 'I know they scored a try because I missed a tackle. Do you think I did it on purpose? What sort of idiot do you take me for? What gives you the right to tell me that I'm crap? So you've never missed a tackle in your life?' Not the most positive line of thinking.

Montpellier, for all the flannel about being a tightly bound group of friends, are quite capable of this sort of back-biting. During one unimportant European Shield game, after a missed tackle had led to a try, our captain, Jérôme Vallée, let fly at the backs while standing under the posts, accusing them of not trying hard enough, while the forwards were working their arses off. Unsurprisingly, this led to a shouting match with Coco, who felt he was the target, and the whole episode did nothing for our much-vaunted team spirit.

Luckily it doesn't come to that as we grind them down up front; the Bayonne pack, difficult to get an edge over in front of their home crowd, seem strangely apathetic, and are obviously suffering from away-game syndrome. A couple more penalties from Coco and another yellow card, this time for Cédric Bergez, Bayonne's lock and captain, yet still we can't score the try that would finish the game. Finally, with ten minutes to go, Lamour gets another yellow card, making his sending-off permanent, and the floodgates open. A number of times I find myself in the unfamiliar role of halfback, slinging the ball wide to our backs, who are carving massive holes in the defence. Two converted tries and a penalty make for an easy-looking 33–0 score-line, and our one regret is that we didn't get the fourth try for an attacking bonus point.

Pau, our next destination, is known as *la ville anglaise*. It became a recreational centre for wealthy English holiday-makers in the nineteenth century, before the nearby resort of Biarritz became more fashionable. Today, its proximity to the Pyrenees makes it a popular centre for winter sports. It is another medium-sized town in the south-west where rugby has a long history: *La Section Paloise*, our opponents today, first played a competition game 100 years ago. The club qualified for the Heineken Cup as recently as 2001 but they have been on the slide ever since, with frequent turnovers of staff and players, and last year had to play off to avoid relegation. (There are no play-offs this year.) At €6.54 million their budget is slightly smaller than ours, and having failed to win a game they are currently placed thirteenth. The game at Stade du Hameau is our first real opportunity for an away victory.

One of the knock-on effects of regularly losing games is that individual confidence often evaporates. Instead of taking the kind of risks that lead to scoring opportunities, players limit their potential for being involved in cock-ups: if you don't take risks you don't make mistakes. Not only does this make for boring games, it is also counterproductive. We are shocking at Pau but so are they—it's not a question of home-and-away. The only charitable conclusion to be drawn is that both teams are paralysed by the high stakes; having finally managed to win a game the previous weekend, we can give ourselves a bit of breathing space with a win, while a loss will have Pau breathing down our necks again.

With the honourable exception of our rugged flanker Cédric Mathieu, the one guy on the field to have a standout performance is Pau's young fly-half, Lionel Beauxis, who plays for the French Under 21s. His siege-gun boot keeps us away from their line, and our inability to string together more than a couple of phases of play does the rest. Pau's driving mauls allow Beauxis to get in range for a couple of drop goals in the first half, and they both fly over from 40 metres. Coco Aucagne, on the other hand, is having a bit of a nightmare. He played most of his rugby for Pau, including during his international career in the late 1990s, and in front of his old home crowd he is feeling the pressure. Still, our incompetence is equally matched by their jitters and it's only 9–6 to them at half-time and then 9–9 shortly after the break, when Coco puts a penalty over, but then they slowly pull away.

I watch the whole *débâcle* unfold from the stands and find it hard to believe that the replacement bench is not being used. Even when, ten minutes into the second half, one of our locks, Sam Nouchi, gets a yellow card for pulling down a *cocotte* (literally a casserole, but in French rugby parlance a maul), I don't get on. More surprisingly, Régis Lespinas, our young fly-half who has also played for the French Under 21s, doesn't get on either. Despite everything, we were still in the game up until the last 20 minutes, and a change of rhythm injected by Régis might have let us sneak a win.

When I quiz our coach Nourault about this afterwards he says he didn't want to destroy Coco's confidence: pulling him off in front of the old home crowd would be potentially shattering for him, and he seems a bit fragile as it is. In my view, Coco's confidence is in a parlous state exactly *because* Nourault spends his time ordering him what to do, and not trusting him enough to make his own decisions. Not taking him off when he's playing badly isn't fooling anyone, least of all Coco, who is experienced enough to understand the situation. At first glance it might look like loyalty, which sounds honourable if a little misguided, but really it's just weakness; because Nourault wants to look like the good guy, he avoids taking the hard decisions. We come away without even a bonus point at 21–12, with all the points for both sides coming from kicks.

Perhaps I am being unfair to Nourault. After all, he has relegated me to the bench and this may be colouring my judgement. Alex Codling, the Englishman who arrived to play lock at the start of the season, has done his back in, and looks like being out of the picture for some time, and Michel Macurdy has broken his hand, so there are only three locks left. If Nourault is not using me now he must have really lost faith in me, even though I thought I did well enough against Bayonne. He has a fetish for line-outs, which doesn't go in my favour: although I am tall enough, I don't have the explosive power you need to jump well in the middle, so I find myself more often in a lifting role. Sam Nouchi is about the same size as me and a better line-out forward, so this probably gets him the nod. He is technically a good player—when I was at Perpignan, Saïsset gave me a list, made up by the French selectors, which ranked the locks in the first division. The division was then made up of 20 teams, so about 80 locks were in competition. Sam was placed fifth, just behind the locks of the national side. (I was thirteenth, which is probably as high as I ever got.) But he often doesn't seem very interested, and in my mind I'm a better player because I want it more.

This is the fifth year I have played under Nourault. I was coached by him in Paris for my last two years, and was captain under him and Jacques Fouroux at Racing. Although it was a difficult time for both of us—results were bad and the club was relegated—we respected each other, and formed something of a bond when we both played significant roles in ousting Fouroux, who was a brilliant ideas man and a highly successful coach (and ex-captain) of the French side, but in club rugby had trouble turning his theories into practice. After I later moved to Perpignan, Norault recruited me for Montpellier, and as I was a senior player he consulted me regularly and listened to what I had to say, even if he rarely implemented my ideas. My 'special relationship' with Nourault, therefore, means that my non-selection, difficult to take at any time, has a sting of betrayal about it.

Sitting on the bench, I have time to make a rough calculation about the game. Montpellier and Pau each have budgets of around €6.5 million, a total of €13 million between them. Both teams play 26 championship games in a year, plus six European Shield games. (The latter are often used as run-outs by teams like us, who know we won't win the competition and are in severe need of a breather from the rigours of the French championship. However, for argument's sake we'll give them equal weight.) There are friendly games and so on, but they are for preparation: the *raison d'être* of the professional team is to perform in the competition. So while hotels and gear and transport costs are included in a club's budget along with salaries, what happens on the field in competition is the end-product: all the time and effort and money poured into a team can be judged only by this.

So dividing €13 million by the number of competition games—32—gives you the value of the money invested by the two clubs in a particular performance: €406,250 or about €200,000 apiece. That is the amount of money being spent on the sorry spectacle we are producing on this particular Saturday afternoon. (True, I don't get the exact figure while sitting on the bench—I have to use a calculator afterwards. But you don't have to be a genius to see that €13 million divided by 32 is quite a lot of cash.)

Money is, of course, the dark heart of the game at professional level. Shamateurism, *l'amateurisme marron*, had been around for years in France, and in most of the rest of the world, before 1995, when the IRB finally squared up to reality after the Rugby World Cup in South Africa. It had become clear that the temptation of big dollars from rugby league and Kerry Packer's World Rugby Corporation was threatening to lure top players away from rugby union's traditional structures, leaving a gaping hole at the top level of the game. The IRB gave its blessing to pay-for-play, and suddenly it was all on as clubs in the northern hemisphere and national unions in the south rushed to make sure they had a legal hold on their talent: contracts.

My first-ever contract was signed with the New Zealand Rugby Football Union in January 1996. Because the NZRFU was still a bit iffy about professionalism, and the legal documents had been drawn up in the scramble of late 1995, it was a contract with All Black Promotions Limited: I wasn't being paid to play, I was being paid to be available for promotional work. This was just window-dressing of course: the sum total of my promotional work was an hour spent in a McDonald's restaurant in central Wellington wearing a Wellington polo shirt and signing (not very many) autographs. No one seemed to know quite what they were doing in the brave new world of professionalism, and at times the whole thing seemed a shambles. Marty Leslie, who later went on to play for Scotland, jokingly pencilled in another three zeros to his match fee for Wellington in the National Provincial Championship. The contract was duly signed and, in theory anyway, he should have been paid a million bucks a game.

Looking back, one of the things I particularly like about that first contract, apart from the feeling that we were getting what seemed like free money, was that there was no differentiation between players. Everyone's Super 12 contract was worth the same, NZ$65,000—$50,000 for the Super 12 itself and $15,000 for the National Provincial Championship. All Blacks were, understandably, a big step up on $250,000.

During my first year with Racing, while playing against Aurillac I had my ear half ripped off at the bottom of a ruck. There was no mistaking that it had been a deliberate act: the ball had already made it out to the backs when the boot went in. As I sat fuming, having the ear painfully sewn back together—repeated attempts to anaesthetise it had not worked as the lobe was so thin the needle kept going right through it—Gerald Martinez, the club president, came in to see how I was. I told him I wasn't being paid enough money for this kind of crap. He asked how much more I wanted. I told him another 2000 francs a month. He agreed immediately. I should have been chuffed about getting a 20 percent pay rise on the spot, but instead I again kicked myself that I hadn't asked for more in the first place.

The point of the story is that it is hard for a player to know how much he is worth. Money is difficult: as Philippe Guillard writes in *Petits Bruits de Couloir*, his excellent book on the vagaries of French rugby: 'If you ask for nothing, you get nothing. And if you ask for too much, you get nothing.'

According to the economics I learnt in the fifth form, the 'market' is supposed to sort out appropriate levels of remuneration. But as I recall (it was a long time ago), to come to the correct conclusion it relies on perfect competition and perfect knowledge, and in rugby this is far from the case. Within the French club scene, teams play each other so often that it is relatively straightforward for a club to assess a player's ability, and decide how much they want to pay him. As a rule of thumb, they find out what he is being paid and offer him a bit more, although this can get a bit complicated if several clubs are interested in the same player.

Young players who look as though they will have a promising career may see big jumps in their salaries. And, of course, playing for France guarantees you good wedge: anyone who has played more than a couple of games for the national side is likely to be on at least €15,000 net a month. On top of this come match fees and win bonuses, as well as sponsorship deals. Certain positions are highly prized because of their rarity—tighthead props, fly-halves and hard-running number eights all fall into this category, along with goal-kickers.

Where it gets really complicated is when players who arrive from overseas are more or less unknown quantities. Star players from big-name international sides are well-known and sought after, even though they are often past their best, take time to adapt to the different style of play in France, and so underperform in the eyes of the uninitiated. A club will calculate not only the added value to the team of having this kind of star player on the field, but also the added revenue in attracting corporate sponsorship and more spectators.

Players like me, journeymen of a reasonable standard but not internationals, and certainly not stars, are hardest to evaluate. Often a prospect will have some Super 14 experience, so the clubs will look at his video footage, but even then it's not easy to tell how a prop, for example, will adapt to French scrummaging, where the laws are supposedly the same as in the southern hemisphere but the referee's interpretation very different. And for a player, the salary he negotiates when he arrives on the French scene will be crucial: barring brilliant performances (or catastrophic ones) it will be the base figure for his time in France.

It could be anywhere between €3000 and €15,000 a month. The current average is around €7000, which is exactly what I'm on. Throughout my nine-year career in France my pay-packet has closely mirrored the average, going from roughly €2000 in 1997 to €3000 in 1998 and 1999, €4000 in 2000, €5000 in 2001 and 2002, €6000 in 2003 and 2004, to €7000 this season. There have been times when I've felt outrageously underpaid, and others when I have felt guilty about getting too much, so the levels have probably been about right.

Ironically, I played my best rugby on about €4000: my performance has decreased as my wage has increased. Partly this is because I was underpaid early on, and partly because budgets have increased exponentially over the last ten years. Partly, though, I have just become better at negotiating.

While these figures are a long way from the multiple-zero-laden cheques that professional footballers tuck into their banks every month, French rugby pays well—nearly four times the country's average wage. From time to time players are unwelcomingly reminded of our privileged position. When I was at Racing, the president, Éric Blanc, informed us that his mother had performed superhuman feats as a nurse working long hours for less than half what we earned. At a training camp at the start of 2007, Alain Egea, the president of the Association—effectively the club's amateur side, comprising youth teams, women's rugby and *l'école de rugby* — told us we were lucky compared to workers in the 'real world', and must always be on time. Montferrand coach Alain Hyardet went to the length of taking his players to the Michelin factory to show them what life was like in this 'real world'.

It is true: we are lucky to be well-paid to play a sport we love, and it doesn't hurt to be reminded of this from time to time. But the implicit criticism that we are spoilt overgrown children puts everyone on the defensive. And there are several counter arguments. For a start, if it's such a doddle, why isn't everyone doing it? And while we are on the rugby field, we are missing out on crucial first steps in the 'real world'; it is not easy to pick up a new career in your thirties, when you quit. The money *is* good. But when we hang up our boots only two or three high-profile players such as Jonny Wilkinson will be able to retire; the rest of us will take up starting positions in the rat race. The lucky ones will have paid off a bit of their mortgage, and the very lucky ones will have made some investments as well.

And then there is the fact that players risk having major injury worries for the rest of their lives. The average office worker may work longer hours for less pay, but he is unlikely to get eye-gouged, or to have to throw himself in the path of rampaging behemoths who want to smash him into the ground and dance on his fallen body.

As a rule, the best way for a player to bump up his salary is to sign a one-year contract, play well, and hawk himself around for the following season. 'What you're on, plus a bit more' every year, as opposed to every two or three years, means the coin starts piling up nicely. Loyalty to a club is not always rewarded by good contracts, and can even be a handicap if, for some reason, you are particularly tied to a region. At Perpignan, for example, one of our players was paid roughly four times as much as another in the same position, even though there was nothing to choose between them on the field. One player had a farm that tied him to living and playing rugby in Perpignan, whereas the other was free to move to the club with the biggest chequebook. No prizes for guessing who got screwed.

The downside to hawking yourself from club to club is the stress. You need to be playing, so other clubs can see what you have to offer. If you are injured, have a run of poor form, or are not playing for some other reason, you will be less in demand and can spend a nervous few months waiting for the phone to ring, watching time tick away to the end of your contract, and wondering where you will be in a few weeks. Every year, there are players who are unemployed at the start of the season. Some never get picked up, while others have to drop a division or two, and find themselves on significantly less cash. Even if you do manage to find a club, there is the scramble over the summer break to find a new place to live, uprooting yourself and your family, and, once there, getting to know a new town and a whole new set of people.

I have often found myself in the role of interpreter in discussions between clubs and prospective new players, and I have seen some interesting decision-making. In my last year at Racing, Éric Blanc took over as president, and just before the season started he got me in to translate in a discussion he was having with two rugby league players from England, John Scales and Jamie Bloem, who had been recommended, in a roundabout way, by Dave Ellis. Ellis is now the defence specialist for the French national side, but in those days he was doing this job for Racing.

There was much small talk, but no light was shed on the men's playing ability, compatibility with the team, or even their passport eligibility. Eventually Blanc said to them in broken English, 'Are you strong? And fast?' 'I can bench-press 130 kilos,' Scales said. 'I can do the 100 metres in about eleven seconds,' Bloem said.

On the strength of this, they were signed up for just over 20,000 francs (€3000) a month plus apartment—1000 francs more than I was getting as an established player. Blanc had assumed that Bloem was English because he spoke English, but it turned out he had a South African passport. This over-sight meant three months' delay getting his paperwork sorted out before he could play.

Racing's organisation was borderline comic throughout that whole year (it was no surprise that we were relegated) but this kind of thing goes on everywhere. In 2005, after a friendly game against the Italian side Viadana, I was having a few beers with Viadana's New Zealand players when one of them, Harley Crane, said that he would be keen to come to Montpellier the following year. We grabbed the president, Thierry Pérez, and asked him if he was interested. Harley, a specialist halfback, had been playing centre that night, so his real game hadn't been on show. I explained this and it didn't faze Thierry in the least. He shook Crane's hand and said, 'Très bien.' It was the classic 'what you're on, plus a bit more' and within a couple of minutes the deal was done. Later, I asked Pérez, an independently wealthy real-estate developer, how he had come to such a rapid decision. It had, he said, been simply a gut feeling.

The people who are supposed to ensure the smooth running of the player-transfer market are the agents. The advent of professional rugby led inevitably to the creation of this particular job, and in the first few years, when the rugby landscape resembled the wild west, there was more than one cowboy getting ten percent of players' salaries for what looked like not much effort at all.

Even today, when things have calmed down, players are inclined to think the price is too high. But a good agent can make a big difference to a player's career, and if he gives his client good advice and finds him the best deal, will more than earn his fee. Agents are better placed than players to know the going rate, and theoretically have the player's best interests at heart since the bigger the player's wage, the bigger their own take.

The problem with agents, though, is finding a good one. I have had dealings with five, and not one has ever been sitting beside me holding my hot little hand when I signed a contract. One got paid but that was a scandal, because his only effort was to give Perpignan my phone number after a former coach of mine, Yves Ajac, had given the Perpignan coach Olivier Saïsset the nod on my behalf. Admittedly, there is an element of self-inflicted injury in my unsuccessful dealings with agents; by juggling various possibilities, and generally trying to be too clever, I have got myself into trouble on at least one occasion.

In 2001, in an effort to rid themselves of the kind of reputation that would make used-car salesmen look like paragons of probity, the more legitimate agents formed a union and reached agreement with the Ligue Nationale de Rugby and the Fédération Française de Rugby. This included an obligation for clubs to use only agents with licences. These licences last three years, and since 2003 agents have had to pass an exam to obtain one.

French law now prohibits players from using more than one agent, but it is well known that some agents have better connections to certain clubs than others, and so the law is sometimes flouted. In 2003, for example, I wanted to play for Stade Français. At the time, and maybe still today, Stade Français recruited most of its players through an agent called Pascal Forni. Another agent, Bruno Xamma, had already approached me with the possibility of going to Montferrand. I preferred Stade Français but I wasn't about to throw out Montferrand in case this didn't work, so I agreed with Xamma that if I went to Montferrand it would be through him, but otherwise I was with Forni.

Forni knew this as well, but he also knew (quite quickly, I think) that Stade Français didn't want me. Instead of passing on this information, he rang Hyardet and told him I wasn't interested in Montferrand, and was only using it to try and gain some leverage on Stade Français. As a result of this Machiavellian move Hyardet and Montferrand went sour.

I should have been stuck back with Forni, who could now get commission on me by selling me to someone else, while he placed another one of his players at Montferrand. But I was unhappy about Forni's dirty tricks—he obviously hadn't banked on Hyardet telling me what had happened—so I made my own way to Montpellier. In the meantime, Biarritz called and made an offer through another agent, Laurent Quaglia, while coming to an agreement with Montpellier not to get an auction going for my services.

If you think this sounds confusing, it certainly made my head hurt. Forni, to give him his due, had a stable of around 200 players, and I suspect my incessant calling got to him. Rugby players waiting for news from their agents are like hopeful young lovers staring at the phone, willing it to ring, and fretting about why their sweetheart hasn't got in touch: coltish and panicky. 'Has he lost the number?' we ask ourselves. 'Has something terrible happened? It can't do any harm if I give him a quick ring, just to see how things are going.' And this, in my case, was three or four times a week over a period of a couple of months.

The year before this I had had uncomfortable dealings with Pau. The club wanted to buy me from Perpignan, who were keen to sell me on. Although I had a year left on my contract, Perpignan had bought two new locks and were happy enough to get rid of me if they could turn a profit. Pau were to pay €25,000 to Perpignan and were supposed to up my salary as well, so I went over to have a look around, meet the president and the coach, and talk about their plans.

David Escloupier, a part-time agent from Perpignan, was handling the negotiations, but he didn't come over with me. No expenses were paid. I drove from Perpignan for four hours, put myself up in a hotel, and although I was to meet with them at nine the next morning, didn't get to see the president, André Lestorte, until after five in the afternoon. By then I was decidedly tetchy, having wasted a day and being about €400 out of pocket.

Lestorte seemed to think the whole thing was a done deal and I would be delighted to come and play for his club. Or perhaps the matter had already been stitched up between him, my agent and Marcel Dagrenat, the Perpignan president, and he was convinced I had no other options. Unhappy about being treated like a piece of meat, I was starting to think just the opposite. The coach was unconvincing, and the clincher came the following day when Lestorte faxed through a written copy of the terms we had discussed. Although we had verbally agreed on €6000 a month, the figure in the document was more like €5000; he had clearly decided to skimp on my pay because he thought I had nowhere else to run.

At this point I no longer had any financial interest in going to Pau, and was sceptical about how the club was going to fare. Meanwhile, though, my agent was encouraging me to go: if I didn't, he wouldn't get paid. Despite threats and cajoling from both Dagrenat and the agent, I opted to stay in Perpignan. Biarritz made me an offer but weren't prepared to pay the transfer fee, and Dagrenat refused to let me go without someone coughing up.

Herein lies a problem with agents. They are supposed to be acting for players, but they are usually paid by clubs. Players don't like the idea of ten percent coming out of their salary—it feels too painful to have to hand a chunk of money you feel is rightfully yours to someone else—so the usual arrangement is that clubs pay the fee directly to the agent, although this is, of course, money they would otherwise give to the player. This means the agents are, effectively, employed by the clubs as head-hunters, and in situations where conflict arises between a player and a club, they will often advise the player according to what the club wants, not according to what is best for the player. In their eagerness to stay onside with clubs, they are, if you like, double agents. While there are hundreds of players, and the pool of talent is constantly being renewed, there are only a small number of clubs, and it is not unknown for presidents to bully agents with the threat of refusing to work with them again if they don't get players to do what they, the club, want.

Brawn and Brains

Brive is a small town of about 50,000 souls in the department of Corrèze in the Limousin region. The town is picturesque, the countryside beautiful (Brive is just a few kilometres to the east of the Dordogne), and the food excellent, but there is not a lot going on—apart from rugby: the stadium seats 15,000 and is often full. The Club Athlétique Briviste Corrèze Limousin, to give it its full name, has been around since 1912 but has never won the French championship, despite making it to the final on four occasions, most recently in 1996 when it lost to Toulouse 20–13. Its big claim to fame is winning the European Cup in 1997, with a comprehensive 28–9 victory over Leicester Tigers.

The following year, having made the final again, they narrowly lost to Bath, 19–18. Internal political strife and a slump in performance led to their being relegated in 2001, but they came back in 2003 with a new president, Jean-

Claude Penauille, who didn't seem to be afraid of putting his hand in his (deep) pocket, and they now have a respectable budget of nearly €7 million, and a team to match. They play in black and white striped shirts, and are currently placed tenth on 12 points, while we are still in twelfth on just five points. The previous week, while we were playing appallingly in Pau, they nearly pulled off a huge upset in Paris, leading against Stade Français throughout the game until crumbling in the last ten minutes.

I finally get to start a game: if I hadn't got a look-in after the débâcle at Pau, the toys would really have gone out of the pram. Playing against Brive suits me perfectly. It's an away game, so we won't be suffering from performance anxiety, and although they play a relatively open style there is a bit of drizzle before the game and the ground is soft, so my aging bones aren't going to have to cart themselves to all four corners of the field trying to keep up with a really quick game.

Their forward pack are not bad but they're not man-eaters either, and I think we can put the squeeze on them up front. We start badly and are trapped in our own territory almost immediately, getting out only after conceding a penalty to their young fly-half, Maxime Petitjean. David Bortolussi does the same for us a few minutes later, and then Petitjean replies: 6–3 after about ten minutes. We are putting pressure on them now. I pick up a ball from the base of a ruck, wrong-foot the defence and get the ball out to Régis, who chips through for Alex Stoica, who duly picks it up and falls over the line. After only quarter of an hour it is 8–6 to us. Petitjean puts another one over, but then their captain, Jérôme Bonvoisin, collects a yellow card. During our ten minutes of fifteen players against fourteen we manage a penalty from Bortolussi, and we go to the break ahead by 11–9. However, we should have cashed in more. To win an away game you can't afford to let slip moments where you have an edge.

As you would expect, Brive come out much more purposefully in the second half, while we seem strangely lethargic. Slowly, they start to impose a stranglehold on the game. Under pressure we give away penalties, Mika Bert sees yellow, and the points start piling up. It is now 18–11 to them. We seem to have blown a wonderful opportunity. With ten minutes to go we kick another penalty, and perhaps the game's not over yet as the pendulum swings back in our favour.

Meanwhile, though, I am in trouble. A few years ago at Perpignan I suffered a stress fracture in my foot. Now, as I try to hold up one of our scrums that has gone into reverse, the injury bites again, and after limping around for five minutes I ask for a substitution. I go off, and Gorgodzilla comes on. He might be just the man for the job as we are bashing away at the line without success; it would be nice to see him fling a couple of black and white jerseys out of the way and go crashing in under the posts. But Brive lost at the death last week and they're not about to let it happen again. Their desperate defence holds up, and we have to be happy with the bonus point. It would be easy to be happy with the bonus— it is, after all, better than nothing—but I am gutted we didn't win. During the long bus ride back to Montpellier we have time to think of the 20 odd minutes in the second half where we unaccountably went to sleep.

If I'm unhappy about the loss, from a personal point of view I'm pleased with the way I played. The good-game gods smiled on me for my return in the number five jersey, and I should start again next week. I had a bit of a run-in with Lionel Mallier, the former French international flanker with whom I used to play in Perpignan; he was a bit dark about my pulling down a maul, but there was nothing in it. It was a scrappy game, neither side managing to hold on to the ball long enough to build up any real momentum, but I was in my element. I would like to be able to tell you that my natural game is haring upfield with the ball in hand, throwing off would-be tacklers with sledgehammer fends, and bamboozling the defence with my crazy-legged running style, but that just isn't the case. I do my thing in the darkness of close quarters, hitting rucks, trying to speed up the recycling of our possession, or slow down theirs, and perhaps snaffle a ball or two, grunt-work in scrums, taking a few line-outs or kick-offs, setting up mauls and making tackles close in, and occasionally out wide, in cover defence. If I get to run with the ball three or four times in a game I'm happy, and it isn't normally for more than a few yards.

From the club's point of view there was also the big positive of successfully blooding a newcomer from the *Espoirs*: Fulgence Ouedraogo, our 20-year-old flanker, was thrown in the deep end and swam like a fish. He is blessed with a remarkable natural athleticism, all lean, rippling muscles, and seems to have discovered the secret of perpetual motion. Lifting him in line-outs is a joy because he leaps like a salmon heading upstream. And, crucially, he has a good head on his shoulders—he's well disciplined, learns fast and runs good lines in support, adapting quickly to rugby at élite level. We should be seeing much more of him in the first team, and there's no reason he shouldn't play for France in the next few years. Of course, all these gifts alone would be worth nothing to him if he didn't work hard at it, and he does.

It is not enough in rugby simply to have physical attributes, although this gives you a head start. Three elements make up a player: physique—basically explosive speed, stamina and strength, although flexibility and balance are also important; technical skills—all-round skills such as catching, passing and tackling, and position-specific skills such as line-out throwing for hookers; and psychological skills—discipline, decision-making and mental toughness.

It is not a question of 'nature versus nurture'. Nature sets the parameters for your abilities—it's no use wanting to be a winger if you run as though you're towing a caravan, or hoping to be a lock if you have to stand on tiptoe to reach the kitchen cupboards. But in truth the physical entry barriers to rugby—at least at club level, if not for international sides—are relatively low, provided you are prepared to train hard. If you start young and are pigheadedly determined to succeed, have access to good facilities and are well-advised, you have a shot. The pigheaded bit is important, because mental strength is at least as important as physical strength.

Professionalism in rugby has led to enormous advances in physical performance as each team and each individual looks to get an edge on the competition. Coaches tend to love fitness sessions and weights tests: the latter are easy to measure, so they can line up a list of figures next to everyone's name and see who is stronger than whom, who is progressing, and so on.

I am not a fan of the weights room—perhaps I would be if I were better at it. In the good old amateur days when this kind of training was optional, I would usually take the easy option. This was a mistake; if there is one thing I regret about my career, it is that I didn't do enough work on basic explosive strength in my late teens and early twenties. When I was eventually forced into a serious weight-training regime, because it was part of my job description, the results were not spectacular (I am known to some French players as '*épaules de serpent*'—'snake shoulders'), but I did gain extra confidence in the contact area, which has become a battleground. When I started playing for Wellington in 1994, offensive tackles were still relatively rare; today a tackle that is not offensive is considered a wasted opportunity.

Obviously, though, strength is useless unless you know how to channel it well. My team-mate, our prop Antony Vigna, for example, is almost as hopeless as I am at pumping iron, but in a scrum I would back him against any of the guys in the team who rack up great rows of 20-kilogram weights, squatting or bench-pressing until the bar sags. Often players —particularly props—who are phenomenally strong in the weights room try to bully their opponents with muscle, ignoring technique, and get themselves in trouble. For these kinds of practical skills there is no substitute for being well coached and then endlessly repeating the same movement, both in training situations and in games, in order to assimilate all the subtle variations you may need to call upon when you're under pressure and the guy opposite is trying to get an edge on you. This is why experience is so highly valued, particularly in the forwards. You can train all you like to do things right—passing, catching, kicking, and pushing are all relatively straightforward to master—but on the field it's what you do in the very short space of time you have before someone stops you doing it that shows whether you're really up to it.

This is where the brain comes into play. What is referred to in New Zealand as 'the top two inches' is without any doubt the most important part of a player's rugby armoury. It's no use having silky skills and a rippling torso if you don't take the right options. Rugby is a relatively complex game, and much of its richness comes from this complexity.

Let's say a halfback has a ball in front of him at the base of a ruck, the sort of thing that happens maybe a hundred times or more in a game. He has to decide what to do from a multitude of possibilities. He can pass it to his fly-half. Or, if he has a big enough blind side, he can decide to change the direction of play by passing it to a winger or fullback. He can pop it up to a forward coming in on the charge, or he can run with it himself. He can try to organise his forwards into a driving maul, or tell one of them to pick and go; or he can choose to kick high into the box for his winger to chase, or hoof it further down the ground for position. He has a split second to decide which of all these options is the best, given the field position of his team, the speed at which the ball is delivered, and the defensive positions of the opposition.

If he has only one defender on him and a hole outside, he may back himself to have the speed to get around him, particularly if the defender is a tight forward. So let's say he goes himself, and makes a half break before being caught from behind. Does he try to stay on his feet to offload a pass to his support, who will run into the breach he has created? If he can do this he will have gained some ground and created forward momentum, which will make it easier to continue the attack. But there is the possibility of a second tackler arriving and trying to rip the ball off him before he can get it away, so perhaps he should choose the relative security of going to ground and setting up a ruck.

You get the picture. Over the space of a couple of seconds he has had to calculate all the various possibilities, decide which is best for the team, and act. Top sides now programme play through several phases after the original set piece, so players are in prearranged positions with their roles mapped out for them. Even so, you still need to be able to adapt your choices to the situation, and the complicating factor of the opposition means things don't always go as planned.

The number of choices are greater for the guy with the ball in his hand, but every player has to be constantly assessing his own actions and maximising his value to the team. In defence, for example, you find yourself on the inside shoulder of a guy who's made a tackle. As a ruck forms, you have to decide: should you go in to try and win the ball and take the advantage for your team? The problem is that, while doing this, you are leaving the other defenders a man short if you don't succeed—a potentially disastrous situation if the ball comes out quickly and your lot have not had time to reorganise.

Even in a maul, which looks like a lot of uncomplicated shoving and sweating, you need to think about the angle on which you are pushing, both vertically and horizontally. If, while defending, you go from down to up, taking an opposition player with you, you are reducing the efficiency of the opposition's driving platform—it is difficult to push effectively when standing up—but you are also less efficient. If you try to force them down you run the risk of being penalised, but if you can make it look as though they fell over themselves you have stopped them in their tracks, and may even recover the ball. You can push them towards the touchline, limiting their options so they are obliged to get the ball out before taking it into touch, or you can wheel the maul towards the open side, forcing the ball-carrier into the open, and a position where he can be tackled. Or, if you like vanilla, you can just try to push straight.

Clearly, no one spends time consciously calculating any of these things. Everything happens so fast you run purely on instincts you have honed over the years, and hopefully some useful advice from your team-mates, who may be able to see things that you can't. (Good teams communicate constantly: players help each other choose the right options by letting others know what is going on around them.)

To be really good you have to consistently make the right decisions, and have the physical ability and technical knowhow to execute them. Deciding to attempt a drop goal from halfway is a good option if you kick it over. But if, like me, you have two left feet and the ball goes spinning off into the arms of the opposing winger, who then scores under your posts, it is a bad option.

During breaks in play there is time for a breather, and a chat with team-mates, where you can reassess your options in relation to your strengths and weaknesses and those of the opposition with a little more lucidity. This analysis is a particularly important task for leaders, and should also have been mapped out to a large extent in the game plan you will have discussed with the coach after watching video analysis.

The other great thing about the human brain is that it can keep driving you forward when your body is starting to flag. Your legs may be full of lactic acid and your head in oxygen debt, but you will continue to perform. This is often described as courage or 'guts', but it is more than that. For a player, courage is simply a prerequisite: if you are playing rugby year-round you can't shirk, because the opposition will quickly start exploiting your weakness. If you turn up to a game thinking you will get by on courage alone, you may get lucky if the other lot are feeling cowardly, but this is unlikely.

So courage has to be supplemented by mental toughness and intelligence. Mental toughness means you are always looking to get more from yourself and your team-mates, setting targets such as holding on to the ball for a given number of phases, disciplining yourself to get a lower penalty count, or staying an extra half-hour at training once the coach has called it a day, because you want to get the preparation absolutely right, not just get home in time for dinner. When you get knocked back by a loss, or being beaten in a one-on-one situation, rather than bleating about the referee or the ball being slippery or generally feeling sorry for yourself, you need to be able to analyse why it happened, and how you can avoid it happening again.

Intelligence, too, is essential. In martial terms, a full frontal assault on the enemy can be described as 'courageous' but it may be stupid as well, particularly if you end up getting slaughtered in front of the guns when a simple flanking manoeuvre would have been successful.

There are any number of great players in world rugby, but while we have some quality players in Montpellier, I would struggle to say, hand on heart, that any are 'great'. One I particularly respect though, because of his hard-nosed attitude, is Olivier Diomandé. I wasn't pleased to see Olivier when I arrived at Montpellier: we had spent an afternoon trading cheap shots in Paris while I was playing for Racing and he was at Nîmes. In those days he was an average prop playing for a below-average side, and his game seemed to revolve around head-butting and eye-gouging. He went on to have a couple of seasons at Bordeaux, then came to Montpellier, which was then in the second division.

Here he started to convert himself into a hooker. He still played most of his rugby at prop, but he wasn't guaranteed a first-team place as a prop. He wasn't guaranteed a first-team place as a hooker either because the captain, Didier Bes, was hooker, but Bes, at 36, was coming to the end of his career, and Dio felt he could establish himself as first choice after Bes left. He was in his late twenties, which is pretty long in the tooth to be looking at positional changes, and he could easily have refused to move, but he threw himself into it, slimming down to become more mobile, practising his line-out throwing relentlessly, and weight-training like a man possessed. He was open-minded and humble about learning from other people, and grew into a key role, playing nearly every game in the last two years.

This year Olivier has been faced with a new challenge: Nico Grelon, an excellent player, has arrived from Perpignan to compete with him for the hooking berth. The two have different strengths: while both are good at bread-and-butter scrummaging and line-outs, Dio does a lot of work in the tight and Nico is more of a ball player. They complement each other perfectly as options, but both want to wear the starting jersey.

Hookers tend to have forceful characters and are often entrusted with leadership roles. These two are no exception, so there has been a good deal of alpha-male rivalry about who gets to be the top dog. There was an illustration of this recently when we were having live scrummaging training— two packs against each other. It is difficult to overemphasise the psychological importance of the scrum in French rugby, and as the keystone the hooker is responsible for the scrum. The two packs were evenly matched, so any slight advantage counted.

As we got ready to pack down for the first scrum, Nico's eight (which I was in) was bound and in position first, giving us an edge in preparation for the initial impact—which is 60 percent of the scrum. Seeing this, Dio started undoing his binding, saying that it didn't feel right, broke up the scrum behind him, and started the whole process again about 30 centimetres off the mark. This is an old trick, seldom spotted by referees; it means the opposition have to either shuffle over on to the new mark, or break up again and reform. Either way, the team that was initially late is now ready first, and so have the slight edge.

As you would expect, there was much moaning about this level of cynicism at training, and I wasn't happy about it myself since we were the ones being disadvantaged. However, Dio stood his ground, grinning, and Nico broke us up and we moved. What I grudgingly admired was that Dio wasn't prepared to cede the slightest advantage to his competitor, even in the relatively unimportant context of training. That is his mindset. It isn't necessarily pretty and he may not be making any friends, but it is effective.

One of the most talented people I've played with is New Zealander Manny Edmonds, who plays fly-half for Perpignan. Manny, whose family moved to Australia when he was six, played for New South Wales in the Super 12 and two tests for Australia before coming to France at the relatively young age of 25. He had more or less blown his chances in Australia by banging down the door of the coach, Bob Dwyer, at five in the morning, after an evening out, to have a chat about why he hadn't been selected for a couple of games in South Africa. Apparently Dwyer was not convinced by his arguments.

Manny, too, is a fierce competitor, although with him it's less obvious because of the sheer joy he exudes when playing. While the rest of us are pounding around the track, running into people and generally slogging our guts out, he is throwing long cut-out passes, dinking little chips through for himself, dummying, then turning on the gas: he seems to be having a great time.

Even the serious nature of professional rugby, and rugby is taken *very* seriously in Perpignan, doesn't seem to curb his enthusiasm. When he first arrived, he would throw the occasional pass behind his back out of the back of his hand at training. Olivier Saïsset, the coach, was unimpressed, and Manny was told we didn't need any of that flashy Super 12 rubbish so he stopped doing it at training. He just did it in games, more out of instinct when he saw a hole opening up as he ran diagonally across field than from outright insubordination, although there was always a hint of this as well. The problem was that often the player receiving the pass was so surprised he dropped it, even though all he had to do was catch it and trundle 20 yards upfield into the space that had been created. (I have a particularly vivid memory of this because I was one of the offenders.) But what was good was that Manny was trying to drag the rest of the team up to his level, rather than reining in his own talent so we could keep up.

Throwing passes out of the back of the hand is pretty banal these days, but what clinched Manny's genius for me was the Heineken Cup final against Toulouse in Dublin in 2003. I was coming to the end of my time with Perpignan. We were rooming together, and on the day of the game we watched the build-up to the Super 12 final between the Auckland Blues and the Canterbury Crusaders on Sky Sports. Stuart Barnes was talking about Carlos Spencer's innovative tactic 'the banana kick'. Spencer would receive the ball from the right and shape to kick left behind the defence, luring the blind-side wing and the fullback across in cover. But the ball would come off the side of his foot—looking as though he had mistimed it appallingly—and bend out on a curve towards the now vacant right wing, where the right winger would stroll through and pick it up.

It was only an hour or so before we were to leave for the ground, so there was no time to practice the move, but as we went down to the team meeting Manny asked our right wing, Pascal Bomati, if he'd seen it. Pascal was enthusiastic and the two of them decided to try it if the opportunity arose. We had a nightmare first half against the wind, for which Manny was partly to blame, falling off a tackle on Jauzion, who went on to feed Clerc for Toulouse's try. At half-time the score was 19–0.

We ground our way back, and with a quarter of an hour to go it was 22–12. We hadn't been able to pierce their defensive wall by orthodox means. Manny got a ball from the right, and shaped to kick left, looking as though he'd mistimed his kick. Everyone was wondering what the hell was going on, except Pascal, who scooted in, picked up the ball and scored. It was a brilliant example of intelligent risk-taking and perfect execution. (Unfortunately it wasn't enough and we lost 22–17.)

Muscles and Magic Pills

Narbonne is another small southern French town with a long history of rugby. Le Racing Club Narbonne Méditerranée has represented its 50,000 people since 1907, and has twice been crowned national champion, in 1936 and 1979. The town itself, situated on the Mediterranean coast, was established in 118 B.C. as the first Roman colony outside Italy. For more than a thousand years it flourished. The Via Domitia and Via Aquitania met here, and this, together with the town's accessible port, made Narbonne an important crossroads. The cathedral and archbishop's palace testify to a thriving past as a trading post and cultural centre, but from the fourteenth century diminished port access for ships due to silting in the Aude River led to a decline in the town's fortunes, and these days the local economy relies on tourism and the surrounding wine country.

Although Narbonne has the smallest budget in the Top 14—only €5.8 million—it continues to hang on, punching above its weight, despite the suspicion it is simply putting off an inevitable drop. Last year the club finished just ahead of us in tenth place, having beaten us in both home and away games.

The first-round game is to be played at Stade Sabathé, Montpellier's home ground. It is important for a number of reasons. First, there is a vital need for us to win and gain four points. Alarm bells are starting to ring, as the championship table currently makes very ugly reading for anyone associated with Montpellier. We have played seven games now for a measly total of six points. And while we were losing in Brive, Toulon beat Bayonne, putting them equal with us, while Pau are only one point behind.

There are also a couple of more emotional reasons. Narbonne is only about 80 kilometres from Montpellier, making this a derby game; they beat us here at Sabathé last year and we haven't forgotten. And five of our players, along with the backs coach, Pat Arlettaz, wore the orange and black of Narbonne before arriving in Montpellier, and games against your old team always have a bit of spice.

From the start, we dominate physically. Narbonne like to play a very open game, so we take them on up front. To try and counter our edge in possession, they live offside. I can't blame them: we do much the same thing when we are being dominated. Dwayne Haare, a big Maori lock who has just arrived from Sydney, is into everything, and we have words on a couple of occasions. There is a bit of pushing and shoving— more handbags at 20 paces than Marquess of Queensberry —but the rest of the Narbonne pack seem more interested in damage limitation. As a result there is little continuity: they either get away with it and stifle our momentum, or are penalised and we kick the points.

Coco is on form, and after 20 minutes we have cruised to a 12–0 lead. Narbonne pull one back to make it 12–3 before Franck Tournaire, the former French prop, gets yellow-carded for taking a scrum down, and the set piece, already going in our favour, becomes a massacre. We kick a penalty to touch, they pull down the maul from the line-out, and we choose to take the scrum. Their pack implodes and the referee goes straight under the posts to award a penalty try.

One of rugby's more esoteric pleasures is being part of a scrum that is destroying the opposition, and nowhere is this truer than in France. You know that every time the referee whistles for a scrum they are dreading the contest, while your confidence is soaring. You still have to work hard for every inch, but they are feeling the pain more than you are: while the pack advancing keeps its shape, the pack in retreat twists and ruptures, as bindings pop under the strain and body positions are contorted. For ten minutes we win every scrum, ours and theirs, and although it might not be much fun to watch, up front we are enjoying ourselves. Nineteen to three at half-time, and it's difficult not to feel that we have broken them.

We exchange penalties in the first few minutes of the second half: 22–6. What was never a great game deteriorates as night falls (all games in the French championship are played in the evening, except for occasional televised matches on Canal+) and the dew makes for difficult handling conditions.

Both teams opt to kick for position and then try to muscle the ball up through the forwards. Narbonne suffer another setback when their captain, Jean-Marie Bisaro, is yellow-carded, and again we exploit our numerical superiority in the forwards when Cédric Mathieu goes over in the middle of a driving maul. A few minutes later, Mika Bert scores after yet another line-out take and drive: 34–6.

Now we can concentrate on scoring a fourth try and pocketing the bonus point. But we are playing in fits and starts, and have lost the edge we had in the scrum. In trying to free up our style of play we get sloppy. Narbonne take advantage of this and score a good counterattacking try. Worse, we are starting to get overanxious as the minutes tick away. I am pinged from the kick-off for tackling a man in the air before he is grounded, and then marched ten yards for holding on to the ball, a stupid error.

As the siren for the end of the game blows we are hot on attack, with a succession of rucks on their line. Time and again it seems inevitable that we will make it over, only to be repulsed by their desperate defence. Harley has come on at centre but finds himself with the ball in his hands at the base of one of these rucks. Our backs change direction and now have a big overlap, but as he goes to swing it wide he sees their defence rush up, so he checks his pass, dummying and scooting inside his marker to go under the posts. But as he dives, a defender comes across in cover and boots the ball from his outstretched hands. It slides away and our bonus point goes with it.

Still, it's a great relief to win, and reassuring that we did it so comfortably. Sam was subbed on for Mika after about 70 minutes, so I played the full 80 minutes, which is something of a personal triumph after the problems I've had with my knee. Over the course of my career I have had plenty of injuries. I've been knocked out several times; dislocated a collar bone; ruptured an eardrum; smashed bones in my hands and feet; broken my nose at least a dozen times; slipped discs in my back; ripped a tendon in my arm; subluxed my shoulder; twisted knees and ankles; had numerous wounds that needed stitching—mainly on my head—and countless bumps and bruises, cauliflower ears and other disfigurements.

Of all of these injuries, my right knee's have been the most troublesome. In 1995 a reconstruction of the anterior cruciate ligament put me out of action for a year. Last year, at training camp, the knee got infected through a tiny cut and I was so run down I couldn't get rid of the infection. After emergency surgery I spent two weeks in hospital, and it was three months before I could play again. And even then the knee wasn't right: the patella tendon, already weakened by the earlier reconstruction, had been partially eaten away, and continually blew up with tendonitis. Only recently, 18 months after the operation, has the knee settled down enough for me to take stairs two at a time; it will probably annoy me for the rest of my life.

This list of war wounds may sound long, but in fact I have been relatively lucky: over 25 years of rugby I have needed only three full-blooded operations (that is, ones performed under general anaesthetic). Scott Robertson, the former All Black back-rower who now plays for Perpignan, told me two years ago that he had had surgery seventeen times, and he may have increased his score since then. And I am still playing. Many players have to stop because of injuries, and every year spinal trauma leaves some in wheelchairs. Unfortunately, smashing up your body is part of the risk you take when you play rugby, although we all prefer not to think about it.

Injuries are the bane of the professional sportsperson's life—up to a point. Career-threatening injuries are obviously a disaster, as is anything that keeps you off the field for more than a few weeks, but as long as your place in the team is secure and you're not missing any really important games, from time to time—say once or twice a season—a little breather with a twisted ankle or a swollen knee can be a welcome respite from the drudgery of training. And while you have time off all the other niggling injuries that have cropped up but been too minor to stop you playing can be worked on by the physiotherapist, or simply allowed to heal.

Perhaps the greatest advantage of this enforced rest is that your mind can wind down. Within a week or two, your appetite for rugby, which has been blunted over the months of intense preparation and competition, returns and you can get back into it with enthusiasm.

If you're really lucky, you have a niggling injury that is considered serious enough to need rest for a day or two more than everyone else between games. Hence, you miss out on the heavier training schedule on Monday and Tuesday, arrive on Wednesday evening for the team run, and by Saturday are raring to go because you feel so fresh. Our centre Rickus Lubbe manages to carry an injury like that for much of the year and, while he is an excellent player in his own right, I suspect this extra recovery time is a major factor in his outstanding season.

Your body is the principal tool of your trade, so the training regime is designed to make sure it is operating at optimum level. There is a delicate balance between doing enough to be at peak form for the Saturday game, and not doing so much that you are knackered. Montpellier's weekly regime varies slightly depending on the circumstances, but typically starts the day after the game with a recovery session at the local pool, and massages from the physiotherapists to work out the aches and pains of the match. (We have three physiotherapists, who rotate shifts so there are always two with the team for training and games.)

Monday morning is the same, with the physiotherapists and the team doctor being available for consultation. Normally we eat together, watch the video of the game, and discuss what happened. The afternoon is taken up with upper-body weight-training and perhaps some running. Tuesday morning it is leg weights and speed-work, while in the afternoon the group splits into forwards and backs so that we can practise position-specific skills such as line-outs and mauls—and occasionally live scrummaging. (Whenever I look over at the backs they seem to be playing touch rugby, but they assure us—the forwards—that they are working hard.)

Wednesday morning is dedicated to an opposition session, and in the afternoon we watch video analysis of the team we are going to play next, run through the game plan, look again at line-outs and kick-offs, and spend the last half-hour on the scrum machine. Thursday is free, although some of the team like to do more weights then, or perhaps on Friday morning.

If we are playing away, we leave by bus on Friday morning, and do some training after we arrive. If we are playing at home, we are free on Friday morning, and then have a light run-through and a few line-outs and kick-offs. On the day of the game we meet for a stretching session seven hours before kick-off (and generally squeeze in a few more line-outs) and then go to our hotel, eat and rest up, before going to the ground an hour and a half before the game.

Different clubs have different variations on this routine, but it is fairly standard around France. Within it there is the question of dosage. How long and how intense should each session be? How much can you ask of the team and different individuals, both in terms of training and games? This is where the coach has to judge the varying needs of the team over the short, medium and long term, consult the physical trainer and, to a lesser extent, the medical staff, and try to come up with the best solution for the group.

There can be tension on several fronts. When it comes to deeming a player fit for service after an injury, for example, the medical staff will err on the side of caution, but if the coach needs this particular player he may try to circumvent them and ask him directly how he feels. Generally players want to play, although this depends whom the game is against—there's no point joining the rush to the front if you're going to get slaughtered. Away games against Paris, Toulouse or Biarritz are not the best way to ease back after an injury. If a player does want to play, he may ask for a jab:

injections of anti-inflammatories and painkillers are rare, but not unheard of. Or he may just hope the injury warms up and he'll forget about it on the field.

When it comes to training, the physical trainer may feel the players are too tired and the volume of work should be reduced, but the coach may think the team needs the extra training and overrule him. And, although it's unusual, you can get tension between the physical trainer and the medical staff, and this is what happens this year.

The first game of the year, against Castres, left a lasting impression on our physical trainer, Nicolas Foulquier. In essence we got bullied by a bigger forward pack, who wore us down up front. Individually, each player seemed to have the advantage of a few kilograms of muscle, and we felt it every time we were in contact. Given that rugby is a contact sport, this is a problem. There are two solutions—either you can buy bigger players, or you can enlarge the existing ones.

Since it was the first game of the season, there was really only one solution. Making players bigger—increasing their muscle mass—isn't easy during a season because there is not much time for heavy weight-training. The weights you do will be more about maintaining strength than progressing. So Nico, in consultation with the team dietician, decided to find the best possible dietary supplement, in the hope we would put on a couple of kilos of muscle and thus become more competitive.

The hitch was that the product he chose, Maximuscle, was English and contained creatine. Creatine is not available in France because the French authorities are not yet satisfied that it has no detrimental side-effects. It is not a question of doping: most of the professional rugby world now takes creatine, and English rugby players appear in some of the advertising. But one of our two team doctors, Bernard Dusfour, was unhappy about players using a substance that had not been given the thumbs-up in France. His argument was that it is easy to lose perspective in the search for short-term results, and his role was to make sure that the players were in good health not only during the course of their rugby career, but after it as well. He put this to the coaching staff, and when they judged that he was being overcautious he resigned. (There may have been more to it than this, but this was what filtered out.)

The players now had access to Maximuscle but we had to pay half the cost, with the club paying the other half. I had taken creatine for a few weeks when I played for Wellington and been sceptical about the results, so being tight-fisted I didn't bother again.

Inevitably, Bernard Dusfour is asked by someone why he resigned. He replies that he didn't agree with some of the nutritional supplements we were taking. A few rounds of Chinese whispers later we are taking steroids. (In French the word is *dopage*, a non-specific, catch-all term for illicit substances.) Rumours of steroid-taking in rugby have been rife for years, and Pierre Berbizier, the former French captain and coach, poured oil on the flames after resigning from the coach's job at Narbonne in 2000. The infernal rhythm of the French championship, he declared, was pushing players to use products that were stronger than creatine: '*dopage*'.

Cue a great wailing and gnashing of teeth by everyone involved in French rugby. If Berbizier had proof of this, why hadn't he spoken up earlier? Who were the guilty parties? Berbizier promptly back-pedalled and said he had just wanted to alert everyone to a *potential* problem. There was no organised doping, but people might be tempted into a 'dangerous spiral'. Everyone calms down, agrees he's quite right to bring such a serious issue to the attention of the rugby world, steps will be taken, case closed.

It would be naïve to think that no one involved in rugby has ever taken steroids. Players looking for a competitive edge are aware of the extra strength and power you can get from illegal drugs, and I don't imagine such drugs are hard to find. A long time ago someone I respected recommended steroids to me. When I looked at him as though he had a forked tail and cloven hooves, he tried to mollify me with a specious distinction: 'Good steroids I mean, not the bad ones.' I was young and idealistic at the time and didn't give it another thought.

Knowing what I know now about the exigencies of professional rugby, and that magic pills and potions may just make the difference between an ordinary career and a good one, would I take them? It's a moot question because at my age it wouldn't make a blind bit of difference. I might look better at the beach (which wouldn't be such a disaster) but it's too late for drugs to have any real impact on my musculature: the body's ability to grow muscle tissue reduces significantly after the age of thirty.

Still, it's worth thinking about the situation that professional sportspeople find themselves in. Apart from the obvious long-term health implications of drug-taking, the danger for a rugby player is that drugs provide a short cut. A game of rugby is more complicated than a 100-metre sprint, or a cycling race where you perform the same action over and over again: pure physical performance is only a part of it. Even if you become stronger physically, cutting corners is liable to make you a weaker person mentally. And just how useful will that extra muscle be? A good weight-training programme, allied to intelligent nutrition, should be preparation enough.

The chances of getting caught should make drug-taking a risky business, but over ten years I haven't been tested once. In France, the rugby authorities take blood samples from all professional players three times a year, but these are to check on the player's health, not to test directly for steroids or other illicit substances. A doctor taking our samples at Montpellier told me that any significant anomalies would be followed up, but it would not be possible to say for sure that you were guilty of drug-taking on the basis of the tests.

Obviously random tests do occur from time to time after a game, although they are not nearly as widespread in rugby as they are in, say, cycling. And these random tests do occasionally find evidence of steroid abuse. Yogane Correa, a lock with the second-division club Albi, was suspended for two years after being tested and found guilty, while Nicolas Couttet, who plays for Brive, was suspended for three months when he was found to have taken an ephedrine-type substance before a game. But for the moment I am sure that rugby does not harbour the kind of widespread organised substance abuse that seems to exist in other sports—cycling, athletics, weightlifting, baseball, American football and soccer, to name a few.

Still, suspicion lingers. Looking at other teams and players who are bigger than you and deciding they are all up to the eyeballs in steroids is a longstanding tradition. When Perpignan went to play Leicester in the 2002 Heineken Cup, I was standing next to fellow lock Jérôme Thion as he flicked through the program notes looking at our locking opponents' measurements. He was shaking his head: 'Look at these guys—two metres tall, 120 kilos, they all run around like rabbits, and they expect us to believe that they don't take something stronger than milk on their cereal?' Jérôme Thion measures 1.99 metres, weighs about 118 kilograms, and has a remarkable natural athleticism that is probably closer to a hare than a rabbit, but you get the picture.

Knowing how hard they have worked to bulk up, players often find it difficult to accept that the competition still seems to be just a little bit bigger. Often this boils down to perception—you get used to your own team-mates and they don't seem as big to you as they do to outsiders, while it is often a bit of a shock to see the other team once they've donned shoulder-pads, boots and headgear.

Even without steroids there is no doubt that, thanks to the extra training that professionalism allows, rugby players are getting bigger and stronger. This has had an unexpected impact on injury statistics. At any given time, of the 600 or so professional rugby players in France about 100 are out with injuries. On the surface, this is no worse than under the old amateur regime, but what has changed is the severity of the injuries. While the full-time medical staff and physical trainers employed by the clubs have managed to greatly reduce the number of pulled muscles and other relatively minor injuries, players are now suffering from more serious problems. As speed and strength increase, the amount of energy released in collisions between players also increases, and although muscle helps stabilise the shock to some extent, the rest of the body—particularly the knee and shoulder joints—is no better equipped than before. Consequently, there is a rise in the number of serious injuries involving ruptured ligaments. It's like an arms race, where the improvement in performance thanks to new technology means you feel stronger and safer—but so does the other guy, and the end result is that you do more damage to each other. There doesn't seem to be any easy solution: no one is about to sign peace agreements.

Stadium Gods

They love their rugby in Toulon. Le Rugby Club Toulonnais goes back nearly 100 years and has won the Bouclier de Brennus, or Brennus Shield, the trophy for the domestic champion, three times, in 1931, 1987 and most recently in 1992.

The town itself, with 160,000 inhabitants—or, if you count the surrounding metropolitan sprawl, more like half a million—is centred around the port. Napoleon Bonaparte first made a name for himself here as a young naval officer by playing a decisive role in lifting the siege laid by the Royal Navy in 1793, and today the French Mediterranean Fleet is headquartered on the *rade*. The stadium is right in the heart of the town, on a site that was a disused velodrome until 1920, when the popular French singer Félix Mayol bought it and donated the ground to the club. The RCT returned the compliment by naming the stadium after their benefactor and adopting his lucky charm *le muguet*, the lily of the valley, as their emblem. Although other clubs have more trophies in their cabinets, bigger budgets (Toulon has the second smallest budget of the Top 14 at €5.86 million) and more stars on their team, there is a popular enthusiasm for the game here that is rivalled only by the Catalans of Perpignan.

The massive spectator support means that playing at Mayol is something of a test of character for any visiting team. Toulon are not having a great year and will probably go down, but if you want to win here you had better be prepared to fight for it—and that's not just a figure of speech. Toulon's first game of the year was against the reigning champions, Biarritz, and they gave the Basques a hell of a fright (and a few bloody noses) before going down 10–20. They are an old-fashioned outfit, playing more with their heart than their brains (home-and-away culture is particu-larly evident—they tend to get hammered in away games) and have been too cautious with their recruitment, but they have a few good players and their forwards are always ready to mix it in front of the home crowd.

The day of our game it is teeming with rain, although this clears just before kick-off. We are in for a shit-fight and we know it. Once again the stakes are high as we go into the game still in twelfth place, just three points ahead of Toulon. If we lose and don't collect a bonus point, we are in the hot seat.

As we arrive at the ground we can see that the way to the normal dropping-off point has been blocked by a crane that is obviously not going to move. Bungle or conspiracy? It's not easy to tell in this part of the world, but I wouldn't be surprised if the locals had decided that a little taste of the Toulon atmosphere in the form of a march through a sea of thousands of red-and-black-wearing supporters would put us in the right mood for the game. The bus driver tries to go around another way but is thwarted again, and at the insistence of our officials he turns into a roundabout the wrong way and ploughs into oncoming traffic, before mounting a traffic island and eventually coming to a halt at the side entrance to the changing-rooms. They'll have to try harder than that to put one over on us.

Still, when we go out to warm up we bear the full brunt of the 14,000-strong crowd—from all the jeering they seem disappointed that we have actually turned up—but at least now we are on the other side of the three-metre-high cage that rings the playing-field. We have talked about not being put off by this, but almost immediately our Georgian prop Mamuka Magrakvelidze starts egging them on, blowing kisses to the stands and laughing. With a few games under my belt I am feeling more confident and slipping back into a leadership role and I bark at him to stop, but the damage is already done—the little bubble we try to put ourselves in to prepare the game is broken. Mamuka likes to show that he is not intimidated by anything—and he isn't—but his provocative gesture is an indication of his individualism, and during the game this individualism is shown up for the costly, ego-puffing exercise it is.

Mamuka used to be a wrestler and started playing rugby relatively late. Because of this, his technique isn't as good as someone who learned the basics much earlier, but his strength and skill in manoeuvring his opposite number in the scrum can be very useful. The problem is that most of his energy goes into this physical battle, and he just doesn't get the importance of teamwork and the interdependent nature of the game. He occasionally forgets line-out calls because they don't seem to be important—he'd rather be proving himself by smashing someone than worrying about the complicated variations we use to win line-outs. But if we lose the line-out because he's not in the right place at the right time, everyone suffers.

Predictably, the match is a mess. We dominate the first 20 minutes, which is surprising because normally Toulon come out spitting fire. They have apparently been given a lecture on discipline, and curbing their natural aggression makes them lose some of their venom. But we can't convert the pressure into points—until the twenty-fifth minute, when Coco puts us into the lead with a penalty, having missed one a couple of minutes earlier.

This seems to kick Toulon into life. Greg Tutard, their centre, busts through our midfield and runs 40 metres before we pull him down. We scramble clear, but they are still on attack. They work a line-out drive from a few metres out, and surprise us by going to the short side. Their South African number eight, Shawn van Rensburg, scores in the corner. The conversion is missed and it's still 5–3 when the half-time whistle blows.

We have the wind in the second half, and start by camping in their 22, but we still can't score. Both sides are tense, the ball is greasy, and the one thing that looks like breaking the deadlock is the scrum, where we are starting to get the upper hand. After nearly 20 minutes, there is still no change to the score. I go in to clear out a ruck—the sort of thing I do twenty or thirty times a game—and as I am trying to shift one of their players off the ball with my right shoulder I feel something like an electric shock ping through the top of my left arm. Straightaway I know this is not good. It's funny how the worst injuries often occur in the most banal situations. There are many times on a rugby field where players crash into each other with such force that you wonder whether they are going to be able to get up, but they just dust themselves off and head off to the next phase. But then, out of the blue, something like this happens.

I lie on the ground, flapping about like a freshly landed fish and feeling sorry for myself. The doctor arrives—at this point Bernard Dusfour is still with us—and I try to tell him what I am feeling. The pain, which was acute for about 30 seconds, has now dropped off. As he tests my arm it seems it may be all right, so I decide to carry on. At the first line-out I detect that this is a mistake: when I try to lift Cédric Mathieu my arm refuses to function.

I cut my losses and head for the shower. In the changing-room I find our president, Thierry Pérez; he is so nervous about the game he can't bring himself to watch. Now that I'm starting to cool down I can feel that the injury is serious, and with my arm hanging uselessly by my side I have trouble taking my gear off. Thierry helps me out in a tender, fatherly way that I find touching—not every club president would be doing this. I give him a cigarette, and as we are both sitting smoking a roar goes up from the crowd. Toulon have kicked a penalty to make it 8–3.

We go out to follow the rest of the game and it's clear that all hope is not yet lost. We are starting to give them real trouble in the scrum, and the referee may be forced into yellow-carding one of their props for repeated offences.

The Toulon pack can feel this, and ten minutes from the end they decide to react. After being shunted a couple of metres, their front-rower Noël Curnier stands up and pops Mamuka, right in front of the referee. It is all they have left, and really it is a gift—the ref is already reaching for his pocket—but Mamuka won't let it rest: he has to go and punch Curnier to even the score. So what might have been a game-breaking yellow card—with only seven men left in their scrum against our eight we would really have them under the cosh, and two penalty kicks in ten minutes would have been perfectly possible—is nullified as they each get one.

To make matters worse, a couple of minutes later Dio cracks and throws a silly punch. Now we are a man down and struggling. The game finishes with us under pressure, and we are lucky to have got away with the bonus point for defence. We are now both tied on eleven points in twelfth equal place, with Pau just a couple of points behind.

The bus trip home is gloomy. My mood is not improved by overhearing a conversation among the coaching staff. If the doctor is right about my injury—he thinks I have ruptured my bicep—I will be out for three months and may need an operation. Alex Codling, the Englishman who arrived at the start of the season to play lock, is out as well—probably for good, as he has chronic back pain and it doesn't look like getting better. Michel has a broken hand and should come back in a month or so. That means three locks out, and if one more goes down we are in serious trouble, so the management are going to buy in a new player. Just when I had made my way back into the team, and with *panache*—Nourault told me after the game he thought I had been playing some of my best rugby—more competition arrives. In the meantime I have to hope the diagnosis is wrong, and that I can recover sooner than expected.

The big game of the weekend is Stade Français v. Toulouse at Stade de France in Paris, and as we make our way back to Montpellier we listen to it on the radio. It sounds a slightly one-sided affair—26–0 for the Parisian side at half-time, before they finish 29–15—but what is incredible is that 80,000 spectators have gone along to watch it. This is a very big deal for rugby in France and, to an extent, rugby in the world. For years rugby has had relatively limited appeal. Its laws make it difficult to follow, and the public, outside the diehard supporters, have found it difficult to get excited about events other than international games and championship finals. But if this many people are going to see a normal club game in the middle of the season, rugby must have a turned a corner, particularly given that France's great sporting rivals, the football teams Olympique de Marseille and Paris Saint-Germain, are also playing this weekend, albeit in Marseille. All week the papers have been full of rugby, and Canal+ has decided to headline its

Saturday night sport with the rugby rather than the football.

Much of the success of this event comes down to the work of one man: Max Guazzini, the president of Stade Français. In the rugby world, Guazzini is an original. For a start he is openly homosexual and you don't see much of that, and although he has never played rugby himself he has a passion for the game and a vision of its potential that has allowed him to build Stade Français from a struggling third-division side to one of Europe's great clubs. Along the way he has turned received rugby wisdom on its head and changed people's perception of the game in France forever.

In 1992, after having amassed a reasonable fortune at the head of French media group NRJ, Guazzini decided to get involved with rugby. Taking over Stade Français in Paris, he immediately democratised the game by offering free entry, first to everyone, then to women and under 18-year-olds, thus building an interest in the sport outside its usual base.

Under his presidency, Stade Français have brought the glamour of show business to the game. Pom-pom girls have become a fixture. So have *Dieux du Stade*—Gods of the Stadium—calendars, featuring glossy black and white photographs of naked, oiled players, together with CDs of songs recorded by players. Such moves show a marketing flair that initially raised a few eyebrows in the conservative rugby world. The knowing flirtation with the homoerotic in the images of well-muscled young men in close physical contact is reminiscent of a Steve Reeves movie, and makes some people uncomfortable. And this year the club unveiled a new pink jersey—another rugby first.

All of this could make Stade Français look a bit silly if they were no good on the field, but they are: they got back into the first division in 1998, won the French championship that year, and have won it three times since.

Guazzini's spectacular success has, inevitably, led to some backbiting. Ticket prices for the game against Toulouse were as low as €5, prompting the president of Paris Saint-Germain to say he could do the same thing several times over if he wanted to. But by filling Stade de France Guazzini proved there is a real market for rugby. Certainly, the razzamatazz of fireworks and a giant karaoke sing-along made for a festival atmosphere, but television viewers also came to the party, with a very respectable 1.4 million watching the game at home.

With this success has come a concern voiced by many of rugby's staunchest supporters, that the game must *garder son âme*—hold on to its soul. It is difficult not to make comparisons with football. Most rugby supporters see the round-ball game as having become decadent and ugly, with widespread corruption, exorbitant pay for players who act like prima donnas, and a general atmosphere of sophisticated cynicism that contrasts with rugby's homespun, down-to-earth values.

Rugby became professional because of a confluence of two factors. The first was a desire for excellence on the part of players and teams; this led to such long hours of training that players felt they should be paid for their time and effort. The second was growing public interest in watching the competition between teams. The motor for change was television: television coverage meant that players could be paid enough money to make rugby a genuine career option.

The success of professional sport is, necessarily, measured by the number of spectators it attracts: more spectators equals more money. Television coverage can enlarge the potential number of spectators exponentially, and so is critical to professional sport. Sponsors know that their names will be seen, not just by the few thousand at the ground, but by people all over the country (and often, through satellite television, all over the world), and television channels pay handsomely for the rights to broadcast matches.

Rugby is an excellent product for sponsors and television companies in the sense that, on a good day, it is both a great spectacle and a vehicle for positive values such as discipline, courage, teamwork and skill. Rugby has been good to television, and television, by and large, has been good to rugby. To accommodate television's needs and make the game more spectator-friendly, rugby authorities have changed numerous rules. At the same time, the presence of cameras has led to a decrease in violent incidents (during televised games, anyway) because players are aware that, even if they avoid getting pinched by the referee or the touch judge, there is a good chance their crime will be played out in slow-motion replays at a disciplinary board hearing, and the camera doesn't lie.

Since the advent of professionalism, rugby has been broadcast more widely in France, leading to an increase in the numbers of people participating in the game, as well as the number of spectators. So everyone is happy: sponsors, clubs, players and television channels are each getting a piece of the cake, and every year the cake keeps getting bigger.

Although this sounds like a wonderful success story—and to all intents and purposes it is—rugby needs to be careful. The desire to appeal to a wider public can result in a game moving away from its roots. Do we really want rugby to be the new football? The problem is that this supposedly independent sport is now, like so many others, dependent on television, not only for reaching a wider audience but also for its revenue. Television is a business, and so all about maximising profit, but the various marketing strategies it employs aren't necessarily good for rugby, or for the individuals who play it.

The most obvious example is the desire to consecrate certain players as stars. In rugby, as in any sport, there are charismatic individuals who stand out. Rugby's interdependent nature, though, means that, no matter how good an individual may be, he can't perform without his team-mates. When, at the end of a game, the 'man of the match' says, 'I couldn't have done it without the lads', he is not just being modest: he is telling the truth. Picking out one player and elevating him above the rest therefore runs contrary to rugby's musketeer-style 'all for one, and one for all' spirit. You may have a great game one week and a disaster the next, but whatever happens you stick with your mates. They stand by you, and you stand by them. That is one of the great pleasures and the great strengths of rugby.

Take the example of Fred Michalak, the young fly-half who was quickly dubbed a genius by the media, and hailed as the French rugby team's version of soccer's Zinedine Zidane. Michalak is a good-looking man (my girlfriend Marion, who is obviously an authority on good-looking guys

115

and a woman of impeccable taste, thinks he looks like a young Marlon Brando) and he was quickly set up as a bright young thing, advertising high-end cosmetics, modelling for Christian Lacroix, and giving countless interviews to the media. He became a highly visible celebrity.

Michalak wasn't complaining, and with people throwing money at him and hanging on his every word you wouldn't expect him to. Unfortunately, though, all this extra attention meant people expected him to perform consistently head and shoulders above everyone else, and like so many 'stars' he was set up only to be pulled down when he showed signs of not living up to his status. During the Six Nations game against Ireland in February 2006 (which France won, despite a 20-minute lapse in concentration that allowed the Irish back in), Michalak was whistled and booed by the public, who were not prepared to forgive an 'off' day from the man they felt owed them a performance in line with his reputation. This prompted Bernard Laporte to defend his player by describing the public as *'bourgeois de merde'*—'bloody bourgeois'—but other commentators made the more reasoned analysis that rugby had become so successful it had acquired a new public, one that wanted a spectacle in line with their expectations, and would tolerate nothing less.

It's difficult to be completely sure who was doing the whistling; perhaps it was the old school giving Michalak the raspberry because they didn't like the idea of a rugby player strutting around on catwalks. In any case, this 'new public' is, of course, exactly the people rugby has been hoping to attract. They are different from rugby's traditional fan base in that they are more spectators than supporters. They come to a game not to show their support for a team, but to be entertained. For them a rugby game is a product like any other, and if they're not satisfied they are unlikely to spend money on it again, whereas the diehard supporters are capable of re-mortgaging their houses to ensure they get season tickets, and are delighted to see their team grind out a 3–0 win if that's what it takes to avoid relegation, or qualify for the semis. I know of supporters who are so nervous they have trouble eating before important games. Like most players I think this is a bit much, but I can remember when I was fifteen sulking for a whole day because Wellington had lost a Ranfurly Shield game to Auckland.

Professional rugby has already made dents in some of the values that the old school, in particular, appreciates. The importing of foreign players has led to complaints from some supporters that they are no longer able to identify with their team, although you don't usually hear much about this when the team is winning.

The relatively new idea of putting names on the backs of jerseys, along with numbers, is an obvious sop to the marketing people. In the old days, either you knew the team well enough to know who the players were, or you didn't care because the only important thing was the colour of the jersey they were wearing.

One of the things that makes competitive sport special is the atmosphere created by the fans. Even if it doesn't change the way you play, it is nice to know that people are intensely involved in what you are doing. In a sense, the difference between the new package and the old is like that between a small French farmers' market and a supermarket: one is all about the values of *terroir*—flavoursome, small-scale and a bit eccentric—while the other is slick and bland but, because of its greater financial muscle, a wiser economic choice.

Customarily, rugby players say little of interest when dealing with the media. Partly this is modesty, but mostly it's wariness: if we let slip something slip in an unguarded moment it may come back to haunt us. The former French centre Richard Dourthe had a moment of honesty in 2000, confiding in a journalist from *Midi Olympique* who had asked him why he had just signed for Béziers. He replied that, while he realised he should say something about being excited about the club's project, working with a great coach or being able to play alongside some great players, the real reason he had signed was because they offered him a truckload of cash and he would have been a fool to turn it down. A few people applauded his honesty, but only a few.

My own initiation to the merits of keeping your mouth shut and your nose clean came in 1996, when I was with the Wellington Lions and we were about to play Canterbury. I was asked on television whether I might be worried about their pack, which was spearheaded by experienced All Black hard man Richard Loe.

'No way,' piped my cocky 24-year-old self, not at all experienced in media interviews, but determined to say something interesting. 'We're not going to be intimidated by Richard Loe or any of the Canterbury team. They'd better watch out for us.'

The Lions' captain, Jason O'Halloran, was with me, and as we left the studio he turned to me and said, 'Jesus, JD, I'm bloody glad I'm not you. I hope Loey wasn't watching.'

What? Holy shit, it hadn't even occurred to me. This is why we are well-advised to limit pre-match press chat to platitudes: don't give the other lot any ammunition. For the record, I didn't sleep well but we did have a good win. Eat that, Ricky. (If you are Richard Loe and reading this book, please bear in mind that this last bit is a joke.)

8

Merchandise

Perpignan is a few kilometres inland from the Mediterranean, on the French side of the border with Spain that is marked by the Pyrenees. Just over 100,000 people live there. So much for the geography. Historically, the town was part of Catalonia until it was ceded to France under the 1659 Treaty of the Pyrenees that ended the French-Spanish war. Ties to the Catalan identity remain strong. Everyone speaks French, but about a quarter of the population also speaks Catalan, and nearly half understand it. At Stade Aimé Giral the signs are bilingual, although this is more of a marketing ploy to target would-be investors from wealthy Barcelona and its region than because anyone might get lost without them.

Perhaps the most obvious cultural link for any visitor is the Catalan flag, which can be seen waving everywhere in the region, but particularly at rugby games. To the uninitiated these flags look red and yellow; in fact the colours are blood and gold. Legend has it that Wilfred the Hairy, Count of Barcelona, was lying wounded after fighting against the Saracens in the siege of Barcelona. King Louis the Pious came to visit him, fresh from the hard-fought victory. Seeing Wilfred's golden shield next to the bed, Louis dipped his hand in the valiant soldier's blood and drew it down the shield as a mark of honour that would be remembered by future generations. This romantic story is almost certainly apocryphal, but it remains a powerful part of the Catalan identity: the symbol of the rugby club is a diamond with four blood-coloured stripes on a field of gold.

The club is known as USAP, Union Sportive Arlequins Perpignan. Originally there were two clubs in the town: Union Sportive Arlequins and Union Sportive Perpignan. The two merged in 1933, bringing an end to a bitter rivalry. In 1923 they had fought each other to a standstill in a 0–0 draw. There was blood on the grass and ten players were sent off.

The Bouclier de Brennus has been to Perpignan six times since 1914, but the last time was 1955, half a century ago. In 2004, USAP made it to the final, following the European final of 2003. They are undeniably in the heavyweight category, even if there is still a notable absence of silverware in the clubhouse.

For me, Perpignan represents the emotional roller-coaster that makes French rugby such a rich experience. I was picked up by the club from the relative obscurity of Racing and had a great season in 2000–2001, the first year of the Catalan rugby renaissance. In 1998 Perpignan had made it to the

French championship final, where they had lost to Stade Français. They had had a difficult couple of years after that, despite making it to the quarter-finals in 1999 after a re-markable last-gasp victory against Agen in the eliminatory round. In 2000–2001 many pundits thought we would go down, but instead we qualified for the Heineken Cup and gave the eventual champions, Toulouse, a hell of a fright, before losing by just a few points in the quarter-final.

Perpignan signed me up again for two years, and both president and coach couldn't say enough good things about me. By the end of the following year my form had dipped and the president, Marcel Dagrenat, wanted to get rid of me, so he warned me that if I stayed I would spend my last season under contract training with the *Espoirs*, the club's second team, made up of Under 23 players, and in all probability wouldn't be on the list of players submitted to play in the European competition.

I stayed on anyway, and nearly a year later, with five minutes to go in the semifinal of the European Cup at Lansdowne Road, I found myself with the ball at my feet, five yards from the Leinster goal-line. I picked it up, ran into the wall of Irish defence, and slipped the ball behind me to Marc dal Maso, who skirted the Leinster pack that was focussed on smashing me, and threw himself over the line to score the winning try. We were in the final. It was probably the high-light of my career. A month later, struggling with an ankle injury that would still have allowed me to play, I travelled to Dublin for the game, only to be told the night before that my services would not be required.

Dagrenet's ruthless attitude did not surprise me. I had arrived at the club in 2000, a few months after him. At that stage, the club was being run by men who were passionate about rugby but had difficulties adapting to the new professional age, and finances were shaky. Knowing of Dagrenat's expertise in this area, a group of ex-presidents and USAP officials had approached him to take over the presidency.

Dagrenat decided to implement what he knew from his experience in the business world. He had made a decent amount of money running supermarkets, and his strength lay in efficiency—extracting maximum value for the least expenditure—and planning ahead to make sure you were carrying the right amount of stock. Obviously this was a good general rule for business, and 'pile it high and sell it cheap' had made more than one man rich. But would it be enough to run a professional rugby club?

At first the answer seemed to be yes. Almost immediately things began to turn around for the good. Dagrenat pulled in new sponsors, increased profits through merchandising deals and opening bodegas at the ground, and generally transformed the club into a money-making machine. But maximising a team's potential requires some understanding of the subtleties of human nature. Over the course of a season each player will have times when he plays less well than at other times. However, given the right conditions he will bounce back. Too often, though, at Perpignan the conditions were not right, and the result was a lot of wasted potential.

Players put terrific pressure on themselves, and should not have to spend time worrying about being thrown out on account of a couple of bad games. Such a scenario can push a player into a downward spiral where, knowing management is lining him up for the chop, he loses even more confidence in himself. Early in my rugby career in New Zealand I went through a bad patch after coming back from a head injury, until Kevin Horan, my coach at Marist St Pats, had a quiet word in my ear. He could see, he said, that I was trying too hard. I was a good player and the ability hadn't gone away—all I needed to do was relax. It was the perfect advice. My self-belief was boosted, and I quickly found my form again.

There are generally 33 players in a squad. Even with a few injured, there are still going to be some who don't get on the pitch, and the better the team, the better the quality of the guys being left out. At Perpignan, though, in the early years of Marcel Dagrenat's reign, there was a rattling turnover. The year I left nearly half the squad was changed, despite the club having made it to the final of the European Cup, something that hasn't been repeated since.

More recently, the club seems to have learned the lesson and there are now only four or five new players arriving every year. However, Dagrenat still seems to think of players primarily as units of merchandise. In an interview with *Midi Olympique* in October 2005, he declared, '*Les joueurs sont notre capital ... quand on a un capital, on le fait fructifier*' ('Players are our capital ... when you have capital you make it yield a profit').

The subtext is that investments that are underperforming need to be jettisoned. This may make sound business sense, but amount to short-term thinking when it comes to rugby. In 2003 Dagrenat brought in several high-profile foreign internationals, of whom perhaps the best known was Daniel Herbert. As a Wallaby centre, Herbert had been capped 68 times between 1996 and 2002, and had been a key member of the squad that won the 1999 World Cup. In addition, he had played 124 games for Queensland.

You don't play that much top-class rugby without incurring a few aches and pains, and Herbert arrived in France with a dodgy knee. The club knew about this, and it was agreed that for his aerobic fitness he would avoid the kind of long-distance running that might inflict wear and tear on aging joints, and replace it with low-impact cycling or rowing. However, this quickly became a sticking point. After Herbert had played, and played well, Dagrenat reasoned that his knee was obviously fine, so he could train alongside everyone else. Olivier Saïsset, the coach, presumably thought that as Dagrenat was not standing by the original agreement to give Herbert special dispensation, there was no reason for him to do so either.

Herbert, unhappy but feeling cornered and not wanting to look as though he were avoiding work, did the training. After a few games, followed by heavy running sessions during the week, his knee had flared up to the point where he had to have time off. After it settled down, he came back and played a few more games, before tearing his hamstring.

At this point, there were already rumblings of discontent emanating from the president's office. Herbert was being paid upwards of €15,000 monthly, and the return on the investment wasn't turning out to be as high as had been expected. Dagrenat was already looking into the possibility of having the Australian declared unfit to play rugby, which would mean the next two and a bit years of his contract would be null and void. Then, as Herbert was coming back from the hamstring injury, he started having problems with his neck. A disc had slipped. The problem deteriorated and in April 2004 it was agreed that he needed an operation.

Dagrenat then set in motion a series of procedures to ensure the club would not have to pay out any more money for a player he now saw as a lame duck. On the day Herbert was preparing to go into hospital for his neck operation (which would fuse two vertebrae together), he was told the club had not processed the necessary paperwork. This was no administrative oversight: Dagrenat told him that he would allow the operation to go ahead only if Herbert agreed to leave the club, giving up the last two years of his contract without any insurance payout or indemnity. Herbert, he said, wasn't fit to play rugby. He had known this when he arrived, and had acted in bad faith when he signed his contract.

Now, I know Daniel Herbert—not all that well, but well enough—and like any of us he has faults (the man is an Australian, for God's sake), but bad faith is not one of them. And it is worth noting that he had had an X-ray of his spine as part of the obligatory medical inspection performed by the club before signing new players.

Determined to prove Dagrenat wrong, Herbert sought the advice of France's top medical specialists and was told that, if all went well, he would be back playing rugby in five or six months, leaving him able to play out the last 18 months of his contract.

He duly had the operation in June 2004. Before the surgery, the right side of his upper body had been virtually paralysed, and for long periods he had been unable to move, or even eat. When he came around from the operation, the right side was better, but something had gone wrong—now his left side was stricken. He battled on. Despite having been barred from using club facilities, he devised a training schedule with the help of his old Queensland coaches, and trained twice a day for six months to get into the sort of shape he needed to return to competition. If he had come for the money, he was staying out of pride, fuelled by the kind of stubbornness that made him a great player.

In November 2004 he felt confident enough to tell the club he was ready to play again. In order to do this, he had to be declared fit for work by a *médecin du travail*, a doctor employed by the French state to decide objectively whether employees were physically able to perform their jobs. He took along fellow Australian Anthony Hill, a kind of camp mother to stray antipodean rugby players. Herbert was still shell-shocked by the way things seemed to work in France but Hill was a veteran, and they were armed with the opinions of the French specialists.

Once they had presented their case and the doctor had made his inspection, he started writing down his findings. Hill saw that he was declaring Herbert unfit to play rugby. He asked the doctor what he thought he was doing, given that all the evidence pointed the other way. The doctor sighed, got up and walked around, then told them that he had had Dagrenat on the phone that morning, and had been told that it was in his best interests to signal Herbert unfit. Dagrenat had reminded him of the influence he had in Perpignan, and was sure the doctor would understand.

At six-foot-six and 130 kilograms, Hill also has not inconsiderable powers of persuasion, and the two men had the advantage of being on the spot. The upshot was that the doctor declared Herbert fit to work.

This would have led to a long stand-off had Herbert's neck not started playing up again just a couple of months later. Medicine is an inexact science, and while the disc between C5 and C6 was all right after the vertebrae were fused, the one between C6 and C7 started causing trouble. From the outside it looked as though Dagrenat had been right all along. Now, after talking to the same specialists, Herbert agreed that he was unfit for rugby. It must have been a sickening blow, and just when he needed support from the people he was playing for when he received the injury, they put the boot in.

There was now no chance of Herbert playing again, and the French state, which had effectively been paying his salary for nine months through work accident insurance, washed its hands of the affair and sent him back to the club, who were legally obliged to offer him some sort of job for the duration of his contract. Dagrenat now made an offer it was impossible to accept: he proposed that Herbert act as his personal secretary, and on game days put ice into buckets, for which he would be paid the princely sum of 5 percent of his previous salary. There would be no negotiated settlement.

To avoid being considered in breach of contract, Herbert was unable to look for any other work until his contract was up, but he decided to fight in the courts, in what turned into a protracted affair. In July 2005 he received an insurance payout of around €200,000. He continued to fight for a payout from Perpignan, and in November 2006 the tribunal awarded him €181,000 in unpaid salary, excluding image rights. He appealed to get the image rights as well, and the club finally settled out of court for an undisclosed sum between €181,000 and €400,000. The upshot was that Herbert ended up with a total of nearly €500,000, nearly three times what he would have been prepared to accept had Dagrenat not been so pigheaded about the whole thing.

This is not the only instance of shifty behaviour on the part of the Perpignan president. He is said to have told player Pascal Meya he would ensure that he, Meya, didn't get a job in the region if he didn't give up the last year of his contract. When that didn't work, he reportedly menaced Meya with a smear campaign in the local press. He tried to get rid of former New South Wales Waratah Ed Carter by saying he would report Carter's girlfriend to the authorities as an illegal immigrant; the club was to have looked after her immigration papers, but stalled when they realised they could be a source of leverage. He has used his contacts to look into players' bank accounts to see how they're spending their money, and engaged in other blatant manipulation.

As well as the financial cost of defending lawsuits, the club's prestige has suffered. The rugby world is small, and word gets around, making potential recruits wary of signing up with a club where this kind of thing goes on. The club's sporting results are still relatively strong, but there is a certain sense of stagnation: it is now three years since Perpignan have made it to a final.

I would like to be able to say that Dagrenat was the only president who operated like this, but it is not the case. At the end of the 2004–2005 season, for example, an outstanding young flanker, Yannick Nyanga, found himself in a difficult situation. When Nyanga, who was born in the Republic of Congo and starting playing for Béziers at the age of 14, signed a two-year contract, the president, Olivier Nicollin, gave him his word that if the club were relegated he would be released without any fee so he could continue playing top-level rugby. Despite Nyanga's best efforts—he played so well he was picked for the French team—Béziers did go down.

However, Nicollin reneged on his word when he realised he could make money by selling the last year of Nyanga's contract. He proceeded to set the dazzlingly high price of €300,000 on a transfer, virtually pricing Nyanga out of the market, and making him very nervous about the possibility that his promising career was about to be nipped in the bud —or, at the very least, stalled for a season in the second division. In the end he was bought by Toulouse, probably for considerably less than €300,000, but some of the money would have come out of what Nyanga would otherwise have been paid.

When you tell this kind of story to grizzled rugby players of an earlier generation, you get the same sort of reaction you get from wide-eyed five-year olds after the first reel of *Bambi*:

a shocked loss of innocence. As Herbert has said, 'You shake hands with someone in the rugby world, and think it means something.' But the modern rugby player is not much more than a piece of meat in the eyes of men like Dagrenat.

Are rugby players naïve to think we can and should be protected from the uglier side of capitalism? After all, we are at the cutting edge of the free market: there are not many other industries where workers move so freely across borders to ply their trade. And rugby is a violent sport. Maybe it's only normal for bad behaviour to spread to the management side? Perhaps it is the entrepreneurial equivalent of eye-gouging?

In a magazine interview, Dagrenat described his detachment from the game. 'If USAP get to the final,' he said, 'I can happily watch it at home on TV ... What motivates me every morning is the economy of the club.' This is disarmingly transparent: he doesn't get any pleasure from the game or the club, but just wants to make sure there is plenty of money.

This isn't quite as worrying as the case of the American multi-millionaire Malcolm Glazer, who bought the football team Manchester United in 2005 for nearly $1.5 billion, largely to offload some of his business debts. But it does raise some questions. Dagrenat has enough money not to need any more, so he's not doing it for the cash; indeed he has reformulated the job description of president to make it impossible for him to be paid a wage. The game itself doesn't mean much to him, he shuns the limelight, and he has at least an inkling that, despite the success that he has brought to the club, he is not well-liked. 'In the rugby world,' he said in the same interview, 'everyone is friendly with each other, everyone kisses each other. No one kisses me. I don't know whether they like me or not, but it's not my problem.'

In late 2005, when it became clear that Dagrenat was introducing several shareholders loyal to him, who would tip the balance and give him influence over more than 50 percent of the club's holdings, several Perpignan officials launched a counterattack. They could, they said, no longer stand by and watch the values of the club they loved being eroded by a man who had no obvious regard for these values. The spat ended with a compromise: the two different sides now hold a total of 49 percent of the shares each, while a block representing supporters and former players holds a swing vote of two percent.

Dagrenat's best defence of his tactics remains the results of the team, and he still has a large number of supporters on his side, who are happy to see their team looking better off than it did before he arrived. The interesting question is whether Perpignan is a forerunner of a new rugby? Is USAP the canary in the coalmine?

In the week leading up to the game I try to train normally. The injury I sustained at Toulon is mysterious: the medical staff can't find anything conclusive on the MRI and scanner results, and the arm works all right 90 percent of the time. However, the physios test it with various exercises and strongly advise against my playing.

Nourault overrules them; he likes pitting players against their former clubs, knowing it gives them extra motivation.

He's right: I feel optimistic and desperately want to play against Perpignan. I decide to try out my arm in the opposition training on Wednesday. It's not great and I miss a tackle because I simply can't hold on, and then we start going backward in the scrum, and as my arm is stretched out and away from my body the pain is excruciating. I can't keep the necessary grip for my binding. Didier Bes is standing next to me as I pick myself up, and I give him an earful, for no good reason other than frustration. It is clear that the arm is not right—it will eventually be diagnosed as a ripped pectoral tendon—so once again I am watching from the stands.

It is a must-win game, and not simply because we are playing at home. We are twelfth equal with Toulon, and Pau are playing Agen in Pau. If Pau win and we lose, they will leapfrog ahead and we will be last equal.

David Bortolussi draws first blood with a penalty after only a few minutes, but after that it is one-way traffic. The ball is greasy, so Perpignan don't use their possession out wide in a way that might really have us in trouble after our Samoan winger Ali Koko collects a yellow card, but they attack intelligently. Nico Laharrague kicks four penalties and Christophe Manas scores a try without our firing a shot. The Catalan supporters, whom I used to love when I was playing there, are crowing, and it is really starting to annoy me. A man sitting right in front of me stands up and waves his scarf at us with a big grin on his face every time they score. I am surprised by how much I want to throttle him with it. At halftime the score is a glum 3–17. We will need a miracle to turn it around.

Eight minutes after the break, our supporters finally have something to cheer about. We work a move on the short side: Bortolussi slips through on a diagonal run and manages to offload in the tackle of the cover defence, flipping the ball up to Rickus Lubbe, who turns on the gas and heads for the corner. Bortolussi converts, and at 10–17 things are looking more respectable.

We wait for the inevitable counter-thrust, but incredibly it doesn't come. The game see-saws back and forth, but another penalty from Bortolussi and we start to think the unthinkable. It is 13–17 and they're under pressure. Ovidiu Tonita, their Romanian number eight, gets a yellow card and we capitalise again, with three valuable points putting us within striking distance. They are not going to roll over just like that though, and they press into our 22 as the seconds tick away. We defend courageously, but we won't be scoring from there.

With less than a minute to go, they set a scrum in a good attacking spot just 20 metres out. It looks as though it's all going to end in tears ... but then they are penalised. I don't know what for, but who cares? We kick to touch up towards the halfway line, win the ensuing line-out and send the ball wide. There isn't much on and we are still nearly 50 metres out, but as the ball comes back across the field, the referee blows his whistle: offside against Perpignan. The siren marking the end of the game sounds almost immediately, but since the stoppage is a penalty we can play it. Bortolussi lines up the ball just inside their half, on the right side of the pitch. He is known as *La machine* because of his metronomic ability to put the ball between the posts, but he has only recently come back from injury and this is on the outer edge of his range. I am so beside myself I can't watch, but the television replays we see afterwards show that he hits it well, and even before the touch judges standing under the posts raise their flags he is punching the air and jumping up and down, celebrating what has to be the greatest comeback since Lazarus. 19–17. The crowd goes wild. I don't even care that I didn't play.

Europe, the All Blacks, the World

Rugby has been played in Agen since 1908, and Sporting Union Agenais has won the Bouclier de Brennus eight times since 1930, most recently in 1988. Agen's 30,000 inhabitants are proud to call their town the prune capital of France. As with many other small towns in the first division, if there were not for the rugby team there would not be much going on. It is beautiful country though, with a well-deserved reputation for good eating, and the rugby team is very good. This is the club that has come closest to breaking the hegemony of the triumvirate of Toulouse, Biarritz and Stade Français in the French championship in recent years, losing 22–25 against Biarritz in extra time in the 2002 final.

The irony of this result was that it came just a few months after Agen had lost 59–10 to the Welsh club Ebbw Vale in the junior European Cup competition, the European Shield. Even the most ardent supporter of Ebbw Vale would agree that this was an unexpectedly large win for the Welsh side, but what happened that day so shocked European rugby officials that Agen were suspended from European competition the following year, the only time this had happened in the history of the competition.

Confronted by a busy calendar, Agen had decided they were going to concentrate on the French championship. Qualifying for the next round of the European Shield would simply add to the pile-up of games to be played, so they decided to throw the game. The problem was that simply losing wasn't going to be enough: Ebbw Vale had to score a barrowload of tries to go through, which meant the French side had to make a meal of it, and they did, waving the Welsh through as though they were trying to free up a traffic jam. They then unashamedly owned up to their ploy in the press, and seemed surprised that disciplinary action was taken. (The penalty was later reduced from a two-season disqualification to one-season following an appeal.) They had cause to regret their action: by finishing second in the championship they would have qualified for the Heineken Cup, but they missed out because of the suspension.

You may be appalled by this exercise in cynicism. Or perhaps you will just shrug your shoulders and figure they made the right calculation, since they got as far as the final six months later. The reality is that this kind of attitude towards the European Cup is not unusual in France. Agen lacked the necessary subtlety that might have allowed the authorities to swallow it: a few yellow cards for repeated technical infringements would have given them much the same result. But every year, when the European competition rolls round after two months of week-in, week-out championship games, one or two clubs will look at the list of wounded, look at the depth of their squad, assess their chances of winning the competition, and quietly pull the pin.

There is obviously a difference between not going all out to win a game and actually throwing it, but it's only a difference of degree, and both run contrary to the nature of any competition. But the clubs know that a full-scale campaign will, at best, tire the players by adding to an already heavy workload, and, at worst, lead to the loss of players through injury, and so the risk has to be worth the potential reward.

This is not to say that the European Cup is systematically written off. It is a great competition for the players because it allows them to come into contact with different rugby cultures, and games tend to flow more because there is less at stake. The kind of negative play that is often seen in the French championship is left behind, and there is more emphasis on attack.

French clubs have a proud record in the European Cup, with Toulouse winning it three times and Brive once, and there have been two all-French finals in recent years. But you need to have strength in depth. Bourgoin, for example, had a bad run in the Heineken Cup in 2004–2005: they lost 0–34 to Treviso at home (the first time a French club had lost to an Italian one in France, and it was a pounding), and topped that in the next round by losing 17–92 to Leinster in Dublin. The reason given for these woeful performances was that Bourgoin (who made it to the semis of the French championship that season, so they weren't there by accident) had put their money into quality rather than quantity of players, and there was a big drop-off in standards when a few key players were rested or injured.

Apart from the three big clubs, and perhaps Perpignan, the rest of the clubs look at the European competition as cake, compared to the bread and butter of the championship. Everyone would like a slice of European success, but only the rich can consistently afford it.

In 2003–2004, Montpellier won the Parker Pen Shield, which sounds quite glamorous but isn't. We qualified by losing our first-round game against Glasgow and slipping down a level. Our rivals were Italian teams who hadn't made it to the Heineken Cup, and had also been knocked out of the second-tier competition. Still, it was fun to win.

It wasn't a great success as a concept though, and no longer exists. Today there is only the European Challenge Cup, the junior brother to the Heineken and with a similar kind of set-up—a four-team pool, with a round robin of home and away games. The winners of each of the eight pools move through to the quarter-finals.

At the start of the year, when we were drawing up our team goals, we discussed the emphasis that would be placed on Europe and decided we would aim to make it to the knockout rounds. This struck me as a little overambitious, given the standard of the other teams. Catania, a Sicilian club, was fresh up from Italy's second division so they probably weren't too flash, but Worcester, even though they had been in the English Premier division only as long as we had been in the

French version, were not going to be easy. And Connacht, the smallest of Ireland's four provincial clubs, would be highly motivated as well. Both Worcester and Connacht could realistically hope to qualify for the Heineken Cup by winning the Challenge Cup, and were sure to take it seriously.

Montpellier, after ten hard games in two and a half months, arrive at the doorway to the European season limping and wheezing like a sick man whose car has broken down half a dozen miles away. Nourault decides this may be a good moment to give the usual starting team a break and let those who have been kicking their heels have a run. It's a good decision. At this stage of the season, after the win against Perpignan but before the game in Agen, we are on 15 points, a nose ahead of Pau. They have 13, while Toulon bring up the rear on 11. We can't afford to lose any more players, and this gives the guys who haven't had much game-time an opportunity to show their talent, and perhaps force their way into the team.

South African Rickus Lubbe and I, the two old crocks, are left off the list submitted to the European Rugby Cup authorities. It will be months before I can play again, and Rickus is being rested. Unfortunately, we don't have the luxury of making the changes in the orderly way you might expect: pretty much everyone who's been playing regularly gets a weekend off or is on the bench, and this doesn't help organisation. A full-strength team, well-prepared and with an eye on the title, might just have had a chance to make it through to the next round.

The mix and match outfit that gets slung out on the field acquits itself reasonably well at Worcester, before going down 18–36 (after 15–15 just before half-time). But we then lose at home to Connacht 13–19, despite putting out a stronger side. The home game against Catania is the one bright spot: they are very ordinary, but we play well enough and keep our heads to win 74–12, which indicates how dreadful the result is when we go to Sicily and lose against them 34–37 a few weeks later. (It seems the more Latin your blood, the more 'home and away' you are.)

We are soundly beaten 10–43 in Ireland, and then lose 21–31 to Worcester at home, so Catania, who beat Connacht in Sicily in their last game, finish ahead of us, and we are dead last. Ouch. So much for qualifying for the next round. However, the beauty of the European Cup is that, even if this cuts at our pride, the wound isn't serious, and while it stings for a bit it soon goes away because we have bigger things to worry about.

The week before the game in Agen we train very well, particularly in opposition. It seems the European Cup experience, even if it not successful in terms of results, may have been useful: our continuity is better, with players getting away good passes in contact. Being less worried about the result gives us the freedom to try things that we might not otherwise, and if we can continue with this confidence in the championship it will add a dimension to our game that has been lacking.

'You play the way you train' is a coaching cliché with which most sides get ear-bashed all the time because it's generally true, but the French are such mavericks that form on the training field is no indication of what will happen on the day. I don't travel to Agen because of my arm, but from what I gather I don't miss much. Agen have had a scratchy start to the season—they are only three points ahead of us before the game, on 18—so perhaps we might sneak a win? A bonus point?

Er, no. Within a couple of minutes of the kick-off they score a converted try, then a quarter of an hour later another one. Dio dots down in the middle of a driving maul from a line-out, and Coco converts with quarter of an hour to go to half-time, but they reply in kind a few minutes later. 7–21 at the pause.

Rupeni Caucaunibaca, their flying Fijian winger, is always a handful (provided he's interested—not always the case) and he assures them of the bonus for four tries shortly after we return. He has a mazy running style, seemingly effortless acceleration, and a swivel-hipped change of direction that would make Elvis envious. All of these attributes combine to make him a nightmare to tackle, particularly if he has a few yards in front of the defence to turn you inside out. Despite the dance routine he's no will-o'-the-wisp, and occasionally mixes it up by simply running over the top of you. Great to watch from the stands, less fun close up. Anyway, it's now 7–28. Coco pulls a penalty back for us but then François Gelez kicks one himself, converts another try and rounds it off with a final penalty. It's 10–41, and definitely no bonus for us.

The result is not much of a shock, and by the time I find out that we have lost heavily I have set up headquarters in an Irish pub, and this eases the pain. I've dragged Marion along to watch England play New Zealand: the All Blacks are on course for a grand slam of the British Isles. Lack of foresight has me also watching the game with Nico Grelon and Drickus Hancke, who are injured too, so I have had to sit through France v. Tonga and Wales v. South Africa to keep them happy. This means nearly six hours of rugby, a considerable investment in what passes for stout in Montpellier, and one stroppy French girlfriend. Happily, the ABs squeak home against the English.

England v. New Zealand hasn't always produced great rugby over the years—historically the Springboks have been New Zealand's leading rivals for world supremacy, although of course the English are, at the time of writing, the current world champions. However, most Kiwis would agree that the one game that New Zealand must not lose is against England.

There is an element of chippiness involved, but it's more than that. New Zealand is often said to have come of age as a nation on the blood-soaked hills of the Dardanelles during the disastrously organised Gallipoli campaign of 1916. New Zealand then numbered less than a million inhabitants, and the Gallipoli campaign landed 8450 men on the Turkish shoreline, of whom 2721 were killed and 4752 wounded. During the whole of World War I, 58,000 New Zealanders were killed or wounded—in a war that took place on the other side of the world.

This may sound strange to self-assured Europeans with thousands of years of history behind them, but New Zealand is a young self-conscious nation with a tendency to judge ourselves by what others see in us, and the massive sacrifice involved during World War I validated the idea that we weren't just a far-flung outpost of the British Empire. We were as good as the Brits, and maybe even better, a country full of courage and resource and natural grit, and big enough to stand on the world stage.

The seeds of this national identity had been sown a decade earlier, when a team representing New Zealand had gone to play rugby in Britain. In 1905 'The Originals', as they came to be known, played 35 games, including five tests, losing only once, 0–3 to Wales. They wore a black jersey with a silver fern, and for the first time were referred to as the All Blacks. The story is told that, in a headline, a newspaper intended to describe the tourists, who were quickly making a name for themselves by allying ferocity with grace, and whose forwards were as skilled and fleet-footed as the backs, as 'All Backs!' but someone slipped in an 'l'. Unfortunately, no one can find a copy of the newspaper, so the more prosaic explanation that the name was a reference to their gear is now generally accepted.

Wherever it came from, the All Blacks beat England 15–0, scoring four tries to none. The men from the distant island colony had beaten the mother country—who had, after all, invented the game—and impressed the British sporting public with their skill and strength. Best of all, they elicited admiring comments from British writers about positive aspects of New Zealand that were reflected in the team's performance: natural, healthy living conditions made them strong and fit, and the egalitarian society made them adaptable, broad-minded and scornful of convention.

All of this tallied neatly with what New Zealanders thought of themselves. New Zealand had measured itself against Britain (most particularly against England, the seat of power) and was proud to have proved its worth. From then on, New Zealand has felt that its place is on top of the rugby world. Losing to *anyone* is disastrous; losing to England is the world turned on its head. The first lines of the traditional haka run: 'Ka Mate! Ka Mate! / Ka Ora! Ka Ora!—'It is death! It is death! / It is life! It is life!'

It is impossible to grow up as a boy in New Zealand without knowing that you are supposed to play rugby and aim to be an All Black. Even before I started, I wore a pair of black pyjamas, with the silver fern over my heart. I was nine when I played my first competitive season, relatively late for a Kiwi kid. We played in bare feet at about eight o'clock on Saturday mornings on the Wanganui racecourse. The pitch was sandy, and in the cold winter mornings it should have been illegal to play without boots, but we loved it.

If the All Blacks have become the personification of New Zealand values, they are also the point of reference for all other sports played in the country. Even the monikers of the national teams in other disciplines are a kind of name check: the basketballers are the Tall Blacks; the soccer team the All Whites; the cricketers the Black Caps; the netballers the Silver Ferns; the yachtsmen steer a boat called *Black Magic*. Athletes, rowers and cyclists all compete in black.

People often wonder how a small country like New Zealand manages to stay so consistently at, or very near, the top of world rugby. There is a raft of different reasons. For example, a large number of the current All Blacks are of Pacific Island origin, and the explosive style of play of these men has allowed the team to keep ahead of the rest of the world in pure physical firepower. But what ties it all together is that the country sees rugby as such a big deal. The older generation, brought up in the rugby tradition, is keen to encourage younger players and pass on what they know.

Innovation has always been part of this tradition. In 1905 The Originals were the first to have specific positions for players, rather than simply lumping large men into the forwards and skinny ones out the back, and each new wave looks for a way to improve. The pyramidal structure put in place by the New Zealand Rugby Union means the whole country is geared towards acting as a feeder system for the apex—the All Blacks—and there is no damaging club v. country tug-of-war over players. Rugby going professional was, paradoxically, inimical to New Zealand's domination, because it levelled the playing-field: players in other countries now had the incentive to put in the same amount of effort.

Of course, New Zealand has gone through bad patches and lost games. And we have won the World Cup only once, in 1987, while our close rivals the Australians have won it twice. But New Zealand has a positive record against every other country in world rugby. Only the Springboks come close—the All Blacks have won just 55 percent of games against them.

I spent my last school year and then three university years in England, and the culture shock was considerable. It would be dangerous to draw conclusions from the rugby I played in the rarefied atmosphere of Eton and Oxford—I didn't do the hard yards in a club, which would have been a better indicator of what English rugby was really like—but I was struck by the attitude of team-mates and coaches. In England, we were 'playing games', which was a healthy activity, and if you won that was great but if you didn't, well, that was all right, because it was the taking part that was important.

I had been brought up on competitive sport, which wasn't quite win-at-all-costs, but nearly. You would be criticised for cheating, for example, only if you were penalised—that is, if you were caught. Sportsmanship meant shaking hands at the end, and wearing the same mask whether you won or lost. In my first match for the Eton First XV, I was threatened with never being allowed to play for them again because I rucked a player who was lying all over our ball. The referee, a Scotsman, didn't blink, but the coaches considered this kind of behaviour deplorable.

Every boy had his own room at Eton, and there were no communal changing-rooms. Just before our first home game, I was stunned to discover that we were supposed to meet the visitors' bus, pick up our opposite number, and escort him to our room to get changed. I couldn't quite bring myself to do this. Once, after we had played Marlborough, a player whom I had been marking refused to shake hands with me, saying loudly, 'I would have enjoyed that game if you hadn't been cheating all the time.' He hadn't left the ground all day in the line-out because I had been jumping off his shoulder, so I felt this was something of a compliment. But what would we have said to each other if I had had to lend him a towel?

Oxford was a big step up from this in every way, but there was still dilettantism in the way things were done, not helped by the fact there was only one official game on the calendar: all the others were friendly matches. The Varsity Match against Cambridge is an anomaly in world rugby, a throwback to the glory days of gentlemen amateurs, when the two universities could field some of the best players in the British Isles. In the professional era it has become something of a sideshow. That said, it is a sideshow that packs 50,000 into Twickenham on a Tuesday afternoon in December, and attracts a television audience of a million people.

The players take the game seriously, but it is the sense of occasion that predominates. The Varsity Match is the last remaining bastion of rugby that bears some resemblance to the intentions of Dr Arnold, principal of Rugby School, and his fellow educators from the nineteenth century: an amateur ethos that is about training young men for life, where the rigour of competition is important, but winning is secondary to larger ideals. I had plenty of fun in my three years with the Oxford team, and made a number of lifelong friends, but the relaxed atmosphere away from the ruthless pursuit of excellence that I had known in New Zealand did not do my rugby any good. I emerged feeling I had gone backwards.

My first tour with Oxford took me to Japan and Hong Kong in 1992. Japan was, and still is, a relative minnow in the rugby world—it is currently sixteenth behind Romania and in front of Georgia on the IRB rankings—so I was astonished to find massive interest in a touring university side. The last of our three games was played against Japan's national Under 23 side in front of 40,000 people. (In Hong Kong, no one outside the expatriate community had seemed interested.)

Rugby's spread around the rest of the world is less obvious, but there are now 95 countries listed on the IRB world rankings. In Sri Lanka there is a 100-year-old tradition of rugby, and schoolboy games can attract crowds in their thousands. In 2005, 40,000 spectators saw the Madagascar Makis beat the South African amateur side at the national stadium in Antananarivo. In Georgia, 65,000 people watched their country play Russia in the 2006 European Nations Cup tournament. Japan has enough money to attract big-name players to its national competition, but poorer countries make do with the resources they have. The Georgians used to make scrum machines out of old Soviet tractors, while in Madagascar children in poor urban areas can be seen using scrunched-up plastic bottles as balls. Finland is ranked 95th of the 95 unions, but has bragging rights to the world's only annual Arctic rugby tournament.

Politics

Biarritz are the current French champions and one of the 'big three', along with Toulouse and Stade Français. The town of Biarritz is tiny—30,000 people—but it is part of the larger agglomeration of BAB (Bayonne, Anglet and Biarritz), which makes up the urban centre on the French side of the Basque country. Since 1998 Biarritz Olympique has been known as Biarritz Olympique Pays Basque—Biarritz Olympique Basque Country—which has caused some consternation in neighbouring Bayonne, where the feeling is that Biarritz are plastic Basques with a lot of money but not much soul. Towards the end of the season someone, probably a Bayonne supporter, steals the 'y' from the stadium sign, so it reads 'Biarritz Olympique Pa s Basque' (Biarritz Olympique *not* Basque).

The town is a former Viking settlement—the Scandinavians landed here in the ninth century and stayed to exploit the fisheries—and its name is said to be a corruption of the original Bjornihus (Bjorn's house) which became Biarnitz, and finally Biarritz. Not that this gives Bayonne anything to crow about as far as Basque names go: it used to be Bjorhamn, then Baionam, then ... well, you get the picture.

Biarritz have taken spectacularly well to professional rugby, largely thanks to the massive sponsorship of Serge Kampf, who may be French rugby's biggest spender through his massive IT and consulting company, Cap Gemini. Serge Blanco, the brilliant French fullback of the 1980s, has also been very helpful. Although head of the Ligue Nationale de Rugby, the administrative body for French professional club rugby, he is more than just a cheerleader for Biarritz Olympique, leading to occasional accusations of conflict of interest.

The result has been that Biarritz, who won the French championship only twice in the last century (in 1935 and 1939), have won it twice in the last five years—in 2002 and 2005—and are odds-on to do it again this year. They were semifinalists in the Heineken Cup in 2004 and 2005, and this year they made it to the final before going down 19–23 to Munster.

So once again we know this won't be easy. Our next game is in Paris, so that won't be any better—we are nearly halfway through the season and we have only 15 points. Happily we are not alone—Pau and Toulon are just behind us on 13 and 12 respectively, Narbonne and Bayonne just ahead on 17. All five teams are at home this weekend taking on the big boys: Pau v. Paris, Toulon v. Perpignan, Bayonne v. Castres. Narbonne have the easiest time of it with a game against

Agen. Depending on the outcome of the other games we could find ourself in a hole if we lose or out in front if we win.

We start by playing into the wind, and from the kick-off Biarritz dominate, using the wind to get into our territory and then looking to score quickly. Actually, it's a little too quickly: they seem to have their eye on the win and a bonus, but they rush and end up making uncharacteristic mistakes. Their knock-ons and kicks directly into touch mean we keep our head above water for a while. But only for a while. In the space of ten minutes their powerful little winger, Philippe Bidabé, scores two tries, Dimitri Yachvili converts one and pots a penalty as well, and it is 0–15, until Coco kicks a penalty for us.

A few minutes later, Mika gets yellow-carded for a high tackle on Biarritz's Argentinian centre, Federico Martin-Arramburu, but Yachvili misses the subsequent penalty and we hold them out, despite being a man down. At half-time it's 3–15, but they look as though they are cruising and will pick up speed in the second half to make sure they get their bonus. We have the wind but fail to make good use of it, and Yachvili makes it 3–18 with another penalty. This is almost exactly the same score that Perpignan led by before we stormed back to win, but I wouldn't be putting any money on that happening again.

Which goes to show what I know: with less than half an hour to go, our winger Lolo Arbo breaks and feeds our other winger, Seb Kuzbik, who barrels over. The try is converted: 10–18. Ten minutes later we kick another penalty, and at 13–18 everyone is thinking of the Perpignan game—can we do it again? With quarter of an hour to go, we have the momentum and Biarritz don't look much like champions. Ten minutes to go and Lolo is well set up by centre Alex Stoica in a two on one. It's now 18–18, with the kick to come. Coco pushes it wide but we still have plenty of time.

As the seconds tick down to the full-time siren, we are still in Biarritz's half. A scrum 40 metres out from their line will probably be the last play of the game. The referee blows for a penalty against us at the scrum. The Biarritz captain, Thomas Lievremont, grabs the ball, takes a quick tap penalty from next to where the ball was put in, and makes a few metres before being tackled by Mika Bert. This is exactly what he was hoping for in taking the penalty quickly: by panicking our defence into tackling him before he can make the requisite five metres (the opposing team has to be ten metres back from the mark where the offence was committed —should the penalty be taken quickly the opposition must allow the ball carrier to advance at least five metres) he gains another ten. The referee whistles for a new penalty near the halfway line, bringing it inside the range of his kicker. This time he gives the ball to Yachvili, as the siren sounds to finish the game.

It is a similar scenario to the Perpignan game, but the boot that will be kicking the ball has the wrong-coloured socks. Yachvili reacts well under pressure. He has played some of his best games for France when the heat was on, while he can look ordinary in less important games. This time he doesn't flinch: 18–21, and the Biarritz players are semi-apologetic as they shake hands, knowing they got away with a win from what was, by their standards, a very poor performance.

At the after-match function, a whisper goes around the Montpellier camp—more among officials and supporters than players—that a great injustice has been perpetrated. Strictly speaking, if Lievremont wanted to take a quick tap he should have taken it from behind his scrum, not from the middle where the ball was being put in. This may sound like nit-picking, but it's important because it would have given us an extra second to get back to an onside position, and we would have been less inclined to panic. So the referee, Christophe Berdos (one of two full-time professional French referees, along with Joël Jutge), should have taken Lievremont back to the mark, where he could play it quickly, or have waited until the scrum had properly broken up and played it on the original mark—that is, in the middle of where the scrum had been and where the offence occurred.

Without the extra ten metres, Yachvili would have been kicking for goal from about 60 metres—not impossible, but pretty unlikely. We would have had a morale-boosting draw and the two points that go with it, instead of a loss and only one bonus point.

Berdos was looking at the scrum and had his back to Lievremont, and it all happened very quickly, so I can understand the slip and I don't think there's any point in getting too steamed up about it. However, quite quickly there is a full-blown conspiracy theory going that we should have had the penalty from the scrum (and referees admit that they are often unsure about what happens in the scrum), that there was an incident just before the scrum where we should have had a penalty, and so on and so on. We wuz robbed.

The conspiracy theory gets juicy when you consider a couple of interesting facts. First, as already mentioned, Serge Blanco, president of the LNR, is a Biarritz man. Any pretence at neutrality was scotched when he was caught giving an energetic pep talk to the team at half-time in the European Cup semifinal against Stade Français in 2005. This was relayed to the television audience by a camera, of which Blanco didn't seem to be aware, in the corner of the changing-room.

Add a pinch of speculation: Berdos has never refereed the final of the French championship. The LNR have a good deal of influence over who referees the final of the French championship, and Berdos, a young man, is naturally ambitious for higher honours.

Finally, throw in a hint of conjecture: Berdos is said to have refereed a game between Toulouse and Biarritz eighteen months earlier that ended with a last-minute penalty for Toulouse, which meant Biarritz lost a game they would otherwise have won. (Actually, he didn't. Didier Mené refereed the game in question, but once the conspiracy juggernaut gets rolling facts get crushed under the wheels.)

Stir over the heat of a narrow home loss, and it's a rich, aromatic brew. However, of the other lowly ranked teams, only Narbonne won their game against Agen, which means we don't feel quite as bad as we might have otherwise.

Thierry Pérez sounds off in the press the next day, although he's clever enough to do so without adding in all the gossipy hearsay that swept across the after-match. I have the opportunity to talk to Nourault and him about the incident in Paris on the Monday after the game. The occasion is the annual *Nuit du Rugby*, a sophisticated bunfight put on by the LNR, Provale (the French union of professional rugby players) and Canal+ after a day of meetings between rugby's various groups. I am there with Lolo Arbo: we are Montpellier's two representatives on Provale.

I put it to Nourault and Pérez that they shouldn't be going public with their criticism: it can give rise to a kind of victim mentality, and legitimise the feeling players often have that the referee has made a mistake. If the club hierarchy starts doing it, you can quickly slide into a situation where players are thinking, 'That's not right,' rather than concentrating on whatever is coming next. Pérez and Nourault's argument is that if you allow bad decisions to occur without making some noise from time to time, referees may unconsciously go against you when a call is 50:50. And it is true that we are a small club and don't carry much weight; referees are more inclined to hear what internationals have to say, and this may not even be conscious.

The fact is, though, that referees have a tough job. Even with the advent of television replays, a decision about, say, whether a try should be awarded is not always obvious. And for a referee on the field, making a call in real-time, with vision often partially obscured, must be incredibly difficult. It's amazing they get it right as often as they do. In France, they do this in an environment that is almost always hostile: the slightest perceived error and the home crowd will give a referee hell. It is not unknown for a referee to be assaulted by irate spectators after a game.

A referee's job is not made any easier by the number of different interpretations open to him. Take a ruck situation where a player from the defending team has tackled the player with the ball, and is now on the wrong side of the ruck and slowing up the recycling for the team in possession. One of the attacking team arrives, and seeing the problem he rucks the man on the floor, and the ball is freed up. In a split second the referee has to make a number of judgments. Is the defending player making an effort to roll away? If not, he should be penalised. If he's lying all over the ball and the defending team have already been warned, a yellow card may even be justified.

On the other hand, is the attacking player simply trying to free up the ball? Or is he gratuitously jumping on his opponent, trying to hurt him? Again, depending how he sees the situation, the referee can let play continue, whistle for a penalty, or even reach for a yellow card.

Often the differences are quite subtle, and one referee will react in a completely different way to another. What is certain is that a referee's decisions have a big impact on the way a game is played. If a referee blows his whistle for the slightest misdemeanour, you may end up with a stop-start affair, which never goes beyond two phases before a penalty is awarded. But if he lets small misdemeanours go and the teams perceive a *laissez-faire* attitude they can exploit, an incident can quickly end up in a boil-over because one lot thinks the others are getting away with it, and decide to discourage them by taking matters into their own hands.

As if this weren't enough, both teams—coaches as well as players—are trying to put one over. From the minute a referee walks into a changing-room to check studs and discuss finer points of law with coach and captain, there are insincere smiles on all sides. Sometimes the chicanery starts even earlier, with press campaigns about how an opposing team cheats in certain situations, and how the referee will have to watch out for certain players, who habitually spend the afternoon offside.

A few years ago the recognition that scrums can be dangerous, and require specialist front-rowers to minimise the risk of serious injuries, led to a new law imposing simulated scrums if there are no front-row reserves left. This was well-intentioned, but open to abuse: if your team spent the afternoon in reverse in the scrum, you just needed a couple of props to go down and your problems were solved. You could bring on a back-row reserve in place of the 'injured' front-rowers, thus gaining an edge in mobility and ensuring you won your own ball in the scrum because there was no longer any competition allowed.

Predictably, this happened quite often. However, the referee had to apply the letter of the law, even if he suspected that teams were not acting in its spirit. And it was almost impossible to decide if someone was faking. Were a referee to tell a prop there was nothing wrong with him, and at the next scrum the player buckled and ended up with a serious spinal injury, the referee could be criminally liable. So this year the law has been changed. Now, if there are not enough specialists for the front row, scrums will still not be contested, but no replacement can be brought on in their place. Curiously, since the new law was put into practice the situation has not arisen.

A referee also has to literally watch where he steps. As he waits for a ball to come out of a ruck or maul he will often stand on the field's open side, on the advantage line between the defence and the attacking team. This means he can see what's happening in the battle for possession, judge the offside line, and be well-placed to get to the next phase. It is a logical position, but it can also be useful for the attacking team because the referee can be used as a screen, blocking the opposition's view of the ball-carrier as he runs into the defensive wall. If you run on an angle at the referee, the player who should be lining you up for the tackle will be partially unsighted as you come towards the contact area, and as the referee steps aside he can block you for a crucial split second, giving you an advantage.

In theory, it should be easy enough for the referee to stay well clear of the action, but if he momentarily checks the offside line, and is then confused by a number of dummy runners coming at him, or perhaps a scissors move—where the ball-carrier cuts with a support runner—he may not know quite where to put himself. And bear in mind that all this is happening very fast. If the ball or the ball-carrier touches him, the referee has to blow his whistle for a scrum to the team in possession, but if he interferes with the defence it's just bad luck. Hence, if a defender feels he is going to be at a disadvantage, he may be inclined to push the referee into the oncoming traffic, on the grounds that he is in the way, and the defender is simply trying to make his tackle. Not much fun for the ref.

Before getting to *La Nuit du Rugby*, Lolo and I have spent the afternoon with the other players' union delegates. I used to think of the union as a useful advocate in any run-ins with your club—for example, Daniel Herbert was represented by it during his legal battle—but in fact it is much more than that. Provale was the prime mover behind last year's *convention collective*, an agreement that guaranteed minimum wages for professional players: €2375 a month for players in the Top 14, with the minimum wage for second-division players fixed at half this rate, exactly the minimum wage for all workers in France; an eight-week break between competition in one season and the next (this doesn't include friendly games or training); six weeks' holiday a year; and at least one day off a week. It has also set up an agency to help retiring players get back into the working world through training and career orientation.

Provale has acquired a sufficiently important role in the French rugby landscape that the traditional clubs v. country wrangle is now a three-way Mexican stand-off—clubs v. country v. players' union. This complicates things, but it is good news for the players. At this meeting, for example, we talk about the possibility of playing games over the Christmas and New Year period, something that has been mooted by the clubs. Their argument is that the calendar is so full we can't lose weekends in the middle of the season without doubling up international games and club games on other weekends, or having to jam three games into ten days, playing Friday, Wednesday, then Sunday. But the players consider the Christmas break sacrosanct. Few live in the same town as their extended families, and it is the one time of the year where they can get together with their family and relax for a few days. Although we have a month's holiday in between seasons, this doesn't correspond with summer holidays for schools and most working families as we are back training by July 14. So, much to the disgust of the clubs, the Christmas break is voted non-negotiable by a large majority.

These kinds of decisions about the calendar may sound boring, but they have quite an impact on how the championship works. Every time an international game is played at the same time as a championship round, the big clubs, which have the highest concentration of international players, are disadvantaged, and the smaller clubs have more chance of pulling off an upset win.

Obviously, the smaller clubs like the idea of doubling up international games and club games (though they don't want to be seen promoting it) because it redresses the imbalance caused by differences in resources. The big clubs hate it because they feel they are being penalised for employing expensive international players. And the Fédération, representing the national side, wants to have the top players available for training and game preparation as much as possible. There is currently even more urgency in their demands because of France hosting the 2007 World Cup: a good performance at home will be a big lift for rugby.

Because the French system, like the English, is not centralised around a national body and side as it is in New Zealand, South Africa and Australia, there is always a certain amount of tension between club and country as the players are the subject of a tug-of-love, and 2007 looks like being particularly knotty. There hasn't yet been an instance of one of the big three clubs missing out on qualifying for the semifinals because they lost a game against one of the also-rans while their best players were on international duty, but if this happens screams of rage will echo round the rugby world, and steps will no doubt be taken.

At the players' meeting we also talk about a medical study taking place on the high number of games played in France, and whether they are dangerous for the long-term health of players. At what point can you be said to be playing too much rugby? Players regularly play more than 30 games in a season—internationals occasionally as many as 40—and with the ever-increasing intensity of the modern game this is worth thinking about: more games and less recovery may start to push players towards performance-enhancing drugs.

It is suggested that the union enforce a maximum number of matches for any one player over the course of a season, but this would be complicated to enforce: coming off the bench for ten minutes at the end of the game, for example, is obviously not as hard on the body as playing the full 80. And you could end up with the ludicrous situation of a player making the final with his team, only to discover that his quota of matches had run out and the union wouldn't allow him to play the most important game of his life.

Enforcing any kind of ruling is difficult: exceptions can always be made, and sometimes the player himself may want to play. At the start of this season, several clubs found that players who had been on tour with the French team were not allowed to play the first game of the championship under the rule laid down in the *convention collective* that requires eight weeks' break in competition from one season to the next. This was despite the fact they had legitimately played friendly games in the lead-up to the start of the season because they were non-official. And the players wanted to play—or at least said they did. (It is difficult to say no.)

Bourgoin followed the rules and didn't play their internationals and lost narrowly at Brive, while Biarritz, Toulouse, Perpignan and Narbonne all played men they weren't supposed to—arguing that they were obliged to because of injuries—and won. They were fined a few thousand euros, which for most of them amounted to being stoned with *profiteroles*. An exception was Narbonne, the poor cousin, who were proud to have Julien Candelon play for France but could ill-afford the resulting €10,000 fine. The players' union now hopes that any infringement of the *convention* will result in a sporting sanction—the loss of championship points—which will carry more weight.

The players' union also has the option of calling a strike. It has never come to that, but before the last game of the previous season there was muscle-flexing and the LNR backed down just a couple of hours before kick-off, when the union threatened a strike that could have been ruinous for everyone concerned: the last round of the season was being played simultaneously by all the clubs and was to be televised.

A strike would have had serious repercussions for the relationship between Canal+ and French rugby. In 1981 TF1, the private French terrestrial channel, was televising the final of the French Rugby League championship live when, after only four minutes, a massive brawl broke out and the referee called the game off, leaving an hour and a half of dead air to be filled. Legend has it that the sport was never again televised. This isn't true, but its reputation certainly suffered. Rugby has worked hard to build a positive media image, and to let down Canal+ would be to shoot itself in the foot. For the players, a strike remains the nuclear option—a kind of mutually assured media destruction. Strike action by professional sportsmen is not unknown, but seldom ends with a victory for the players.

For all the occasional disputes between the clubs, the players and the Fédération, the relationship is still a healthy one. Most of the key figures are former players themselves, and know how to settle their differences over a beer. I run into Serge Blanco, Franck Belot, the director of Provale and ex-captain of Toulouse, and Jacques Delmas, the coach of Biarritz, at about three in the morning in a Biarritz nightclub after our return game, and they are looking as though they get on all right.

For the Stade Français game in Paris I am still out with the ripped tendon, but I go up to watch. Stade Français have a fascinating past. In 1892, in the first-ever final of the French championship, they lost 3–4 to Racing, but the following year they won the championship, and they went on to win it eight times between 1893 and 1908. Then in 1927 they lost to Toulouse in the final, and the next 60 years were spent in the wilderness—until Max Guazzini took over the reins in 1992, amalgamating the by then third-division club with the nearby Club Athlétique des Sports Généraux (CASG) in 1995, and installing Bernard Laporte as head coach the same year.

In the next three seasons Stade Français won their division and gained entry to the next, and in 1998 they beat Perpignan in the final and were, once again, French champions, 90 years after their previous title. They won again in 2000, 2003 and 2004, and have twice made it to the final of the European Cup.

Bernard Laporte became the French coach in 1999, but retains close links to the club. He was followed as coach by George Coste, who was ousted during the season. The players then ran the show themselves for two months, and remarkably won the championship. Then came Australian John Connolly, who seemed to have problems adapting to the French mindset. Nick Mallett, the former South African coach, followed in 2003–2004 with more success, no doubt aided by an understanding of both the language and the national psyche, acquired when he played club rugby in France during the 1980s. Fabien Galthié, the former French captain, is the current coach.

The Parisians put out a side close to full strength, but have the luxury of leaving a few of their usual first-choice players on the bench. They shouldn't have too much trouble beating us, and their only real worry is scoring four tries to ensure they come away with the maximum five points. Within five minutes they have scored a converted try, and it looks like being a long, uncomfortable night for Montpellier. We hold our own for a while and even make a few holes in their defence—particularly from counterattacks—but we can't finish. After David Skrela has added a penalty, Jérôme Vallée cops a yellow card and Stade Français score again almost immediately. It is 0–17 and we've been playing only 25 minutes.

Montpellier were annihilated here last year 82–12, which was in some sense revenge for the 49–25 kicking we gave them when we played them at home. Let's hope we're not going down that road again. David Bortolussi kicks a penalty, so we go to the break with three points on the board.

Shortly after the restart they turn over possession to us in our half. We use it quickly on the short side, and Seb Logerot, our young utility back who is playing on the left wing, sets off on a darting run, turns his marker inside out and sprints all the way to the line. It is a peach of a try, and when Bortolussi converts it's 17–10. A couple of minutes later he kicks a penalty: 17–13.

The score against Perpignan was 17–3 at half-time before we turned it around. Surely that can't happen again? For a short while it looks, incredibly, as though it might, but then reality kicks in. Bubu gets a rather dubious yellow card, and in the ten minutes we are a man down Stade Français score twice, pocketing the bonus and putting the game out of reach.

With a little more than ten minutes to go, Jérôme boils over with frustration about another debatable call, and insults the referee to his face. Cue yellow card, which, because it is his second, becomes a red, and he is off for the rest of the game. Again Stade Français score twice, and wrap the game up 45–13. We spent just over 30 minutes of the game playing with 14 against 15, and during those 30 minutes they scored five of their six tries.

Food and Fire

First thing after the Christmas break we play our return match against Castres. I am injured again. If you are starting to worry about the fragile physique of the author, you're not alone. I hope you won't consider it giving the game away if I tell you that I do get to start a few more games during the season.

This time around I watch the game on television. By the time I switch it on, five minutes after kick-off, we are already seven points down. Uh-oh. Then Lolo Arbo burgles an interception: 7–7.

Our scrum starts to dominate in Meeuws' absence—even ex-All Black props get injured—and Coco kicks a couple of penalties: 7–13. Castres score again, but we are still in it at 14–13, driving a line-out into the in-goal, for what must surely be a try. But Dio, our hooker, seems to put the ball down on someone's foot, not grounding it properly, and then it spills forward, and the referee gives them the scrum.

Castres recover while we go to sleep for 20 minutes, letting three tries in and effectively losing the game.

When the half-time whistle blows it is 35–16, we are a man down after Jérôme Vallée has been yellow-carded, and any chance of a win has vanished. In the second half the game loses its structure, as often happens when the result is a foregone conclusion. Castres, having already scored four tries, have pocketed the bonus point for attack and are now just going through the motions. Another interception, this time from Seb Logerot, and then a well-constructed second try for Arbo mean that, with 20 minutes to go, we too can start to think of a bonus point. But a quarter of an hour from the end our tighthead prop, Antony Vigna, collects a red card for a wild swing of a punch that doesn't even connect but is right in front of the referee, and at 14 against 15 we just don't have the fire-power.

Antony is, in one sense, a prop of the old, old school. If Gorgodzilla looks like a grizzly bear, Antony is more like Big Ted, a roly-poly type who has made no concession to weight-training programs or dietician's directives over the course of his career. He is a good friend of mine, and his dedication to *foie gras*, cheese and extra helpings of all the good things French cuisine has to offer, combined with an enduring obsession with progressive rock from the 1970s and internet-based role-playing games, make him a particularly endearing character. Even if he is, by some distance, the least athletic person in the team (for which I am grateful, because otherwise I am the backmarker), he is a very effective player, who uses his bulk intelligently. All the shortcuts—or, as an old coach of mine used to say, 'the fat man's tracks'– are well-trodden paths to him, and the dark arts of the front row are an open book. However, he is not usually given to punching people without reason.

Antony's action is a sign of our collective frustration that we should have let slip a winnable game so badly that it became a 54–28 hiding, coupled with the fact that he got clattered high and from the side while standing quietly on the side of a ruck minding his own business. Still, we try to accentuate the positive. It was, after all, an away game against a good side, and 20 minutes of good rugby is better than none at all.

The home and away thing is, of course, not the only surprise for foreigners new to France and its rugby. One of the first things that struck me was the food. This, after all, is France, so food is important. For my first game at Racing Club we met four hours before kick-off to eat a three-course meal together, followed by coffee. I enjoy eating, was brought up to eat everything on the plate, and the food wasn't bad, so I tucked in and finished whatever was put in front of me. I may even have asked for seconds. It was only later, as we made our way out to the ground, that I realised that my digestion was never going to have time to cope with all that food between now and when we started the warm-up.

Adrenalin does funny things to the body, and I have played enough rugby that I need only walk into a changing-room, smell the liniment, and hear the sound of steel sprigs on concrete floors, and a Pavlovian response kicks me into so-called 'fight or flight' mode, even if I'm not playing.

Adrenalin shuts down your stomach and sends all the blood to your muscles and brain, which is ordinarily quite a useful thing, but not when you have just got through three courses with all the trimmings and coffee, and are starting to wonder whether you will shortly become reacquainted with the chicken and pasta you thought you'd seen the last of an hour ago.

I don't know how everyone else coped. Maybe they were used to it, or maybe they hadn't made such pigs of themselves as I had. In any case, my French wasn't up to discussing the problem and I had to start worrying about the game. My alimentary canal, though, wasn't going to be ignored, and as we started going through the drills there was a succession of perps, parps and hoots that would have put an oompah band to shame. Contrary to belief, the French enjoy toilet humour at least as much as the English, so if there was no sympathy I had at least made some of them laugh. By half-time everything had calmed down, but it was not a performance I would want repeated.

The other thing about pre-match food is that the menu is always the same. *Always.* That was my first taste of ham and *crudités*, followed by chicken and pasta, topped off with yoghurt or *fromage blanc*, and if I'd known it was going to be the same meal before every game for the next nine years I might have held off.

The quality of chicken and pasta varies, of course, depending on where you are. Italy is at the top of the table. Some parts of France are better than others—there is a little place just outside Castres where the chicken is always roasted with thyme and lemon juice—but the food is generally trustworthy.

England and Ireland, too, are all right. In fact, England was the one place where the infernal cycle of chicken and pasta was broken for me: once, in Gloucester in November 2002 (trust me, you remember these things), for some inexplicable reason we broke with tradition and had bacon and eggs as brunch before an early game.

Scotland and Wales, on the other hand, are infamous among French rugby players for being gastronomic hellholes. Admittedly, sampling has not been exhaustive, but the chicken always seems to be boiled an unearthly pink and borderline unidentifiable, and while pasta is not an easy dish to cock up, they seem to manage it.

'You are what you eat' is an old saw, and as professional sportsmen we are often reminded of the importance of diet. Most clubs have dieticians who intervene on a regular basis, and Montpellier is no exception. Over the years we have all heard the speech about complex carbohydrates, and branch amino acids, and fruit and vegetables, and no alcohol and certainly no tobacco. Everyone nods piously and asks a couple of token questions, but the reality is that the message falls on stony ground, in France anyway. In every club in which I have played at least a third of the squad are regular smokers and pretty much everyone boozes, although not to Anglo-Saxon proportions. Everyone eats pasta, even though, as All Black legend Colin Meads recently pointed out, if pasta is so good for rugby players, why aren't the Italians world champions?

Just recently our dietician tried to get across the message that, physiologically speaking, we should be eating big meals at lunch but lighter dinners. Laurent Arbo made the comment afterwards that this was a message that would be hard to get across, given the social importance of a good meal and everything that goes with it at the end of the day. As he said this, he was miming popping the cork on the evening bottle. So there is still work to be done.

Another thing for which France is justly famous, but perhaps less proud of, is its bureaucracy. The state seems to be everywhere, and for anything to be done all sorts of mind-numbing forms have to be signed in triplicate, and various pre-conditions satisfied. The trick is to get someone who knows how the system works—or, better still, the people who run the system, as I saw early on with Racing Club. My new coach, who had used a translator for contract negotiations, picked me up when I arrived, and predictably proved to speak excellent English. The '*je ne parle pas anglais* but if I have to I know a few words' line wasn't the only French cliché that went according to type. We dropped my gear at a hotel and then went to the offices of the Fédération de Rugby to start sorting out my licence. I was arriving in mid-season, after the cut-off date for signing new players, but he didn't seem fazed by this. Brandishing a box of chocolates for the secretary who would be looking after my dossier, he said, 'Here in France we know the rules, we understand the rules, but'—with a Gallic shrug—'we break the rules.'

Unfortunately, this kind of efficiency wasn't shared by

everyone at Racing and I spent the whole of my first year without a work permit—not because I couldn't get one, but because I had been reassured that I didn't need one.

Perpignan, my next club, was the same happy mix of annoying formalities and well-intentioned corruption. Shortly after getting a car from the club I picked up a parking ticket, and knowing by then how things worked I decided to mention this to one of the helpful club officials. He was embarrassed by my question (I suppose I was hinting that I wanted something done about it), not because I was implying that he might be able to help me with something dishonest, but because it seemed to him to be so self-evident that parking tickets should not be paid off but dealt with through the proper channels—that is, by someone who knew the right person to talk to. He was genuinely put out by the fact that, as he explained, he wasn't able to help because his usual contact had recently quit and the new guy was less helpful. The new man was from somewhere else, and didn't understand the way things worked.

In February, the week before our return game against Bourgoin, I have another close-up view of the bloodthirsty nature of French rugby players and decide not to get involved. Coming back from injury (still) I have to tog out with the Bs. The captain is our young hooker, David, who is 21 and a fiery little bastard hell-bent on proving himself. He's not a bad player, but today his tactical decision-making leaves a lot to be desired. I make a quick calculation and realise that I was playing for the Wanganui Under-14 rep side around the time he was born, and can't decide whether I find this amusing or terrifying.

I am playing alongside Drickus Hancke, the new lock recently arrived from South Africa and ex-captain of Eastern Province, who is also feeling frustrated. As we roll up to another line-out and David makes another debatable call, I hear Drickus mutter under his breath, 'That's right buddy, throw the dice.' I keep trying to make helpful suggestions based on the wisdom of my considerable age, but keep being told, '*Non, ce sont les consignes*' ('It's the game plan').

This does little to improve my mood. We are playing against the second team from Auch on a Sunday, and it's been a long week. Training with the *Espoirs* on Wednesday is a grim affair well out of town on a dodgy potholed pitch, and culminates in a game situation against *les Reichels* (the Under 21s). If the *Espoirs* are, as they are sometimes described, a swarm of Killer Bs when playing against the first team, the Under 21s are like a school of piranhas against the *Espoirs*: if you look at them individually they are not particularly intimidating, but as soon as you have the ball in your hands you have about six of them gnawing at your leg. And there seem to be about fifty on the pitch.

Anyway, this particular Sunday afternoon we are beating Auch (whose first team is in the second division) but there is nothing very impressive about the way we are doing it. We are under pressure in the scrum but nothing serious. We are comfortably clearing the ball, but David is unhappy because the props are boring on him and he makes the executive decision that I should *relever la prochaine mêlée* ('lift up the next scrum')—that is, drop my binding and reach through and punch one of their front-rowers.

I have done this a couple of times, but only on special occasions when we are really getting pasted. I am not about to do it in a Sunday afternoon B game that we will win at a canter, just because someone's pride is being dented. I don't want anyone to get hurt—least of all me, particularly as it would be well-deserved: no one takes kindly to getting popped in a scrum while they are defenceless, and there's a good chance that it would kick off a *bagarre générale*.

All-in brawls are much more fun to watch than to participate in. What I try to do in these situations is keep my back to our side and make sure I don't get outflanked by anyone. The sneaky prick who blindsides you tends to do much more damage than anyone fighting face-on, and my reach tends to make sure no one gets close enough from in front to land one. Wading valiantly into the fray like some latter-day knight in search of honour, glory and justice for all may seem like a good idea when the adrenalin is pumping and the blood starts singing in your ears, but really it's a mug's game. In the unlikely event that you connect with your target you will probably get a red card, but there's more chance of getting clubbed yourself, particularly if you're on your own—and you probably will be. The best you can reasonably hope for is to flail away for a bit, firing warning shots across people's bows, and taking a couple of light grazes that will show up well at the after-match to remind everyone that you don't mind getting stuck in. This strikes me as not much of a reward for a hell of an effort and considerable exposure to danger.

If you're really getting pummelled, grab the guy nearest you and pull his head as close to yours as possible, while holding on to him so he can't head-butt you, and snarl something suitably belligerent that will make him think twice without encouraging him to go berserk. (Suggestions of cuckoldry are best avoided in France, being the one insult guaranteed to goad the target into a blind rage.) That way he can't hit you, and his mates are unlikely to try because they may miss you and hit him, and with any luck it will all be over quickly.

Whatever you do, don't go down. Kicking people in the head is an absolute disgrace and contrary to all the unwritten rules, but you never know just how crazed some of the opposition may be. Sometimes your team-mates can be just as scary. I have a lasting memory of a *générale* in Perpignan, when we were playing against Bourgoin, and one or two faces on our side with big grins obviously revelling as boots went flying in, and Sebastian Chabal racing in to swallow-dive into the middle of the fracas.

While everyone probably prefers to play in games that don't descend into brawls, it is difficult not to be nostalgic about the brawls after the fact. Generally people are no more seriously hurt than they are while playing the game normally, and you can have a beer afterwards and talk up your own performance outrageously with your mates. Some people will think that sounds mad, but most people who have played rugby in France will understand.

Soon after I arrived in France I was genuinely moved by something that happened to me in what could have been a very ugly situation. Racing Club were playing in Montpellier in a cup game. I tackled a guy who was running straight at me across the chest with my shoulder—the sort of thing that had happened a lot in New Zealand and that I considered perfectly legal. However, I timed it particularly sweetly so his feet went flying out from under him and he spilled the ball forward and landed flat on his back with a satisfying grunt, and my tackle may have looked a bit high.

I fell next to him and was surprised to have one of our players jump on me almost immediately. I understood when I felt a hail of kicks thud into his body—he was covering my head with his torso because he had seen a horde of nutters descending on me. He must have taken five or six solid blows to the back, but he just got up and said, '*Ca va, mon ami?*' As I dusted myself off I saw it was our hooker, Carlos Martos. I haven't seen Carlos for nearly ten years now but I would happily buy him a beer any time he likes. Without getting too bleary-eyed, I find it beautiful that someone, particularly someone I didn't know well, would do something so selfless for me. (Footnote: The referee, after roundly remonstrating with everyone involved, penalised me.)

The return match against Bourgoin turns out to be one of our better games. My miserable outing with the *Espoirs* is not enough to get me back into the team, so again I am watching from the sidelines. Bourgoin score one beautifully worked try from a set piece, but they are without Benjamin Boyet, their linchpin at fly-half, and Papé seems below his best before going off, and by squeezing them in scrums and line-outs we prevent them building anything. With half an hour to go, it's still close at 23–20, but a converted try and a penalty allow us to pull away to a comfortable 33–20 win.

'Should I Ever Need You'

Y ou can see the bell tower of Bayonne's Gothic cathedral from the middle of the rugby field. Historically, *l'esprit de clocher* meant that anyone who lived within earshot of the church bells was supposed to uphold the honour of that town in the traditional sport of *la soule*. *La soule* is one of rugby's ancestors, a game played between two villages on holy days and fêtes, and written evidence of it dates back to the twelfth century. Each side aimed to manhandle a ball made of leather or an animal's bladder into their own goal, be it a wall, a tree or a body of water. The exact origins of the game are murky, but there is a suggestion that it was linked to pagan fertility rituals: unlike rugby or football or most other modern sports where you go forward to attack the opposition's goal, in *soule* you wanted to take the symbol of the sun or the harvest or the child-bearing properties of their village back to yours.

181

That seems to have been the only rule. As to how you got the ball or bladder there, you could kick it, throw it, carry it, but of course the thing was to get hold of it. The sport was often bloody. With no rules to police, and no one to police them anyway, injuries were commonplace and deaths not unheard of. Once the game had been won, the recipient of the *soule*—probably an innkeeper or the local noble—was obliged to put on food and drinks for the victors as recognition of their valour on behalf of the village.

These bacchanalian festivities were not well-regarded by the *bourgeois élite* in place after the French Revolution. They preferred order and good sense from their workers, and over the course of the nineteenth century *la soule* was gradually stamped out. The spirit of the bell tower, though, lives on. A hardy few are even attempting to revive the ancient game, and in recent years matches have been played around France, although more in the spirit of organised fun than for village honour or the harvest gods.

Britain had similar games of 'folk football' through the Middle Ages, while in Italy Florence had the famous *calcio*, which, despite being a sport where you could handle the ball, has now lent its name to their football championship. In fact, ball games with goals were played all over Europe—and the world. The Chinese had *tsu chu*, and the pre-Columbian South Americans had *tlachtli*, although handling was not allowed in either game.

As far back as 800 B.C. the Greeks were playing *episkyros*, while Julius Caesar kept his troops fit playing *harpastum*. So the idea that William Webb Ellis was the first person to pick up a ball and run with it is romantic but misguided. There can be no doubt, however, that the modern game was refined in the English public schools and universities, where various forms of football were played. Rugby split from Association Football in 1863, and the Rugby Football Union was founded in 1871. The following year the game arrived in France via English merchants and sailors, and the first club, Le Havre Athletic, was set up by Britons in 1872. The same year saw the founding of the English Taylors Club in Paris—Brits again. Racing Club de France and the Stade Français were formed by French students in the 1880s and the two clubs competed in the first-ever final of the French Championship in 1892 (Racing 4, Stade Français 3). The referee was a certain Pierre de Coubertin of Olympic Games fame; he would also referee the first full French International against New Zealand in 1906.

It was under de Coubertin's aegis that rugby was played at the Paris Olympics in 1900. It was then played in three more Olympics and the reigning champions are the United States, who in 1924 in Paris beat the French 17–3 in the final. (Romania was the only other team entered in competition.) The game was a vicious affair, with players knocked out and sent off, and apparently two Frenchmen simply walked off at half-time, sickened by the violence. At the end of the match the crowd rioted, and some of the American spectators were set upon. The whole affair was considered not very Olympic-spirited, and rugby disappeared from the games.

Until 1899 the French championship had been open only to Paris clubs, but that year provincial teams were allowed to compete. Stade Bordelais beat the Parisians of Stade Français 5–3 in the final, and the power base of French rugby shifted south to what is still the rugby heartland. If you draw a line across the middle of France from La Rochelle in the west to Lyon in the east, of the thirty clubs in the professional divisions (Top 14 and Pro D2), only the two Paris clubs, Stade Français and Racing (now Racing Métro), are north of the line.

Rugby grew quickly in popularity, cemented by the French accession in 1910 to what then became the Five Nations. However, in 1931 France was suspended from the tournament following suspicions of professionalism, excessive violence on the field, and the introduction of rugby league, the amateur code's professional cousin. League drew spectators and players away, and the 15-a-side game slumped, until it was given an unlikely shot in the arm by Marshal Pétain during World War II. Certain rugby union officials close to the Vichy regime exercised their influence to eliminate the competitor by having *le jeu à treize* banned, its assets stripped and its grounds taken over, with players given the choice of playing union or nothing at all. Although rugby league was unbanned after the war, it never received compensation and has struggled ever since.

The English, though, can't afford to feel smug about French rugby's unsavoury connections. Just before the war, George Orwell wrote that 'a bomb under the west stand at Twickenham on international day would end fascism in England for a generation.'

Why did rugby take off in France when cricket, say, did

not? The other major nations of the rugby-playing world—the foundation members of the International Rugby Board —are all 'home' nations (Britain and Ireland) or former British colonies with similar values and a shared cultural heritage. The English public schools and universities where rugby was codified into a sport were a far cry from the popular enthusiasm of the *Midi*, where rugby was taken up *en masse*. In England the game had developed under men—such as Dr Arnold at Rugby School—who wanted to formalise elements of education that couldn't be learnt in the classroom. Strength, stamina, teamwork and physical courage were seen as important to a class of young men who were to make up the officer class of the British Army, and run the vast empire that Britain had acquired. The idea behind this 'muscular Christianity' was that military virtues were framed by discipline and respect for rules. In this context, rugby was considered character-building. Baron de Coubertin, when he encouraged Parisian students to take up the sport, was thinking along the same lines: he had been inspired by what he had seen during his numerous trips to England.

But in the South of France, the attraction was not so much the building of character as the expression of identity. The Olympic creed—'It's not the winning, it's the taking part'—reflects de Coubertin's idealistic view of sport as generating moral virtues simply through participation. Try telling that to a Frenchman playing in a derby game between Quillan and Limoux, Bayonne and Biarritz, Lourdes and Tarbes, or any one of dozens of small towns bristling with parochial pride, and full of old scores to settle with their neighbours or their big-city cousins. They would sweat blood—and didn't mind spilling a bit—to ensure victory. Rugby clubs around the world all treasure their pride in the jersey, but the deeply rooted nature of the French population in the south made it particularly fertile ground for a game that was a vehicle for expressing the better qualities of their menfolk in an inclusive, egalitarian group that drew upon the special skills of individual members. The combative, physical nature of the game lent itself to a reinforcement of bonds that were almost tribal.

A couple of weeks before the return game against Bayonne, I call Nourault and ask him if he will be wanting to take me. If not, I plan on having a weekend off. The game with the *Espoirs* did little to help me back into the team, and I tell him I don't plan to spend the rest of the season—in all probability the rest of my career—playing second-string rugby. He says the other locks are playing good rugby, and should he ever need me he'll let me know in advance.

The good news is that this means a weekend off. The bad news is the phrase, 'Should I ever need you...' I tell him I feel great, having been able to spend a couple of months doing weights on my legs, and that I am not so old I am ready for the knacker's yard. And I performed pretty well in a recent friendly game against Castres. 'Of course, of course,' he laughs ominously. Shit. I used to be pretty high up the food chain. In my first year, despite carrying various niggling injuries, I was rolled out every weekend, bar one when I was too sick to play. Last year, despite complications with my knee that demanded constant running repairs, I was assured of a starting spot. I hadn't realised how vertiginously steep the downhill slope would be.

It's no consolation, but I am not the only one feeling frustrated. Our Argentinian flanker Martin Durand is the one guy in our team of genuine international class. *Midi Olympique*, the French rugby newspaper, recently conducted a poll among international rugby writers as to who were the best players in the world, and Martin placed equal with Schalk Burger and Joe Rokocoko, and just ahead of Carlos Spencer. No one else in Montpellier comes close to rubbing shoulders with those kinds of names. Yet Martin has played only a handful of games and has spent more than his fair share of time in the *Espoirs*. His form has not been as good this year as it was last year, when he was quite extraordinary, and he has had problems with his back, but he has had a gutsful and is apparently applying for a transfer.

The return game is billed as a must-win affair for both sides. Although we have managed to build an eight-point cushion between us and Pau, in thirteenth position, we are still twelfth on 25 points. Bayonne are just ahead of us on 26. Logically, there is no reason we shouldn't win. We won here last year in similar circumstances, and if we were 30 points better than them in September surely things haven't changed that much?

Bayonne look jittery at the start, making several unforced errors, but we are unable to do anything right so after an initial period of 15 minutes, where both sides feel each other out, Bayonne slowly take control. Individually and collectively we are disastrous. The score of 16–0 at half-time becomes 44–0 with ten minutes to go, and we look like finishing the game without even firing a shot, until our reserve halfback, Harley Crane, comes off the bench to play flanker after our promising young back-rower, Louis Picamoles, goes down with a dicky knee. Crane takes a tap penalty, and runs through virtually unopposed to score from 30 yards out. Bayonne are just going through the motions now, and at the death Anthony Vigna bustles over for a score, Coco converts and the score is a slightly less humiliating but nonetheless highly embarrassing 44–14. Not having been involved myself, I won't pretend I lose any sleep over it. If you looked closely, you may even have seen the flicker of a smile when I heard the result.

It had been hoped that the return game against Bourgoin was a turning point but it now seems a distant memory. The home-and-away mentality explains some of the gap between the September and February results, but we are talking about a 60- or 70-point difference, and you can't attribute all of that to a change of venue and a bus ride.

Much of the blame for our sloppy performance is, therefore, laid at a convenient door. An article in *Midi Olympique*, published the day before the game, had said Montpellier were to get a new coach next season and this is said to have *destabilisé* the team.

The rumour mill about the coach has been in full swing for a while, and is probably good news. Nourault seems to have run out of ideas—or rather, he has spent the last few weeks casting around for new ideas, done the rounds of what might work without really giving it a chance, and, having reassured himself that he was right all along, has come back to the dead-end street we were going down in the first place.

Alain Hyardet's is the name most often mentioned as a replacement. Hyardet was successful with Béziers, although he then had a disaster at Montferrand, where he was sacked early in his second season because the squad was underperforming. By all accounts he wasn't solely to blame, but the spectacular success of his replacement, Olivier Saïsset, didn't do his reputation any good. The gist of the *Midi Olympique* article is that Hyardet will be coming to replace Nourault, and there will be several new signings across the board. This is what really starts tongues wagging—the mercenary is intensely conscious of the precariousness of his situation, and that anyone can be swept out by the arrival of a bright new broom who will inevitably want things done his way.

To try and calm everyone down, on the bus going to the game Nourault and Pérez talk to the team, saying nothing is finalised and you can't trust the press, but they are looking at signing new players, and coaches are being interviewed as Nourault will be taking a step back into a more managerial role. Predictably, this fails to calm anyone: it is effectively confirming what was said in the paper. There is a widespread feeling that the presence of smoke tends to indicate flames somewhere underneath, and everyone is wondering whether their arse is going to get burnt.

However, most of the guys are signed until at least the end of the next season, and there is widespread agreement that we need a new coach. So, why all the fuss? This sort of thing happens all the time in professional sport, where results are paramount; it is, after all, a business (of sorts) and the bottom line is that anyone underperforming gets chopped. Seeing the speculation in print, I suppose, brings it out of the realm of idle gossip and crystallises fears. It is one thing to stand around griping about the coach and the way we play—in fact, it's almost part of the job description—but you need to be careful what you wish for, because you might just get it.

The truth is that we are a conservative bunch. 'If it ain't broke, don't fix it' is the mindset. But the team itself rarely gets to decide when it is 'broke'. There is a natural loyalty to your fellow players that makes you view with suspicion the idea of new recruits. New 'in' means old 'out' and you might be one of the old. In my first year at Perpignan, when we were hoping to qualify for the Heineken Cup, I remember one of the players saying that we would be better off *not* qualifying, because qualification would mean that the club would have more money and, being ambitious, would sign up flash new players and we would end up being surplus to requirements. I was a key part of the team at the time and I thought this was rubbish, but he was right. We did qualify, as Perpignan have qualified every year since then, and four years later only two of that group are still playing for Perpignan.

Davids v. Goliaths

O ur return game against Toulouse is played the same weekend that France play England, depriving Toulouse of their six French international players. There is a good deal of wailing and gnashing of teeth on the part of coach Guy Novès that the game is being played at all, but it has already been delayed once because of a clash with the Six Nations program, and there is simply no more room in the calendar unless we play on a weekday.

It is worth pointing out that Toulouse are missing merely their *current* internationals: in fact there are still twelve players in the starting line-up with international experience: nine for France, and one each for New Zealand, Ireland and Argentina. Not too shabby, then. At the same time, Toulouse have suffered over the past couple of months from what seems to be fatigue, with most of their squad on call for international duty of one sort or another, as well as the European Cup and French Championship. They have lost a couple of games they would have normally expected to win, particularly a shock home defeat against lowly Bayonne. So we think there may be the sniff of a chance.

The French king Henri IV was, apparently, rebuked by his confessor for his sexual liaisons outside his marriage to the queen. His response was to order that the priest should be given nothing to eat but partridge. 'Toujours perdrix'—'Partridge again'—was the lament of the man of god when confronted with the same rich feast night after night. I have eaten enough chicken and pasta to know what he was talking about: professional rugby has you playing so many games throughout a season and over the course of a career that playing top-class sport in front of a crowd of thousands becomes a humdrum affair.

However, the match against Toulouse is my first game back after four months out with the ripped tendon in my arm, and even though I am only on the bench I revel in the whole thing as though coming to it for the first time: the training session the night before in atrocious conditions, where we don't drop a ball through the 45 minutes; the comfortable intimacy of sharing a room with a team-mate; the slow build of adrenalin as we get closer to kick-off; the precision of the line-out drills in a nearby park the morning of the game; the uncanny silence of the bus ride to the stadium with everyone in their own thoughts; the feel of the ball in your hands and the smell of the grass underfoot during the warm-up; the first sharp thuds of contact with flesh and bone as the intensity of preparation increases; the rapid sentences, full of expletives, that are spoken earnestly by the group's leaders in the changing-room as the minutes tick away. In between, players' backs are slapped, bums tapped and encouragements murmured, small gestures of affection that would probably be inappropriate anywhere else but which I find strangely moving. Several guys tell me how pleased they are to see me back.

As always, we gather in a tight circle with our arms over each other's shoulders and look each other in the eye as a few final words are said, the referee's whistle blows and we file out, steel sprigs clicking on the concrete floor, towards the tunnel, and the noise and colour of the arena. As I take my seat on the reserve bench, 'Carmina Burana' is at full throttle on the loudspeaker system and the drums of the Toulouse fans are thudding a slow martial beat. I love every minute of it and the game hasn't even started yet. It makes me realise how much I have missed it, and how much I will miss it when I stop.

Believing you can beat Toulouse in Toulouse is a triumph of optimism over experience, particularly for a 'little' team like ours. The problem is that if you don't believe, if you go there simply out of obligation and think more along the lines of damage limitation, you will get slaughtered. They can put 50 points on you without even playing particularly well. I remember going to Toulouse with Perpignan the year we made it to the final of the European Cup. They put 40-odd points on us and we didn't even feel we had played badly. Last year the tally was 60 points, all done without even making it hurt. Unlike other teams that beat you up before sending the ball wide, so you have physical bruises to go with your psychological ones, they were able to score several tries from first phase without having a finger laid on the ball-carrier. The irony was that we scored four tries ourselves, largely through driving mauls from line-outs, and so came away with a bonus point for attack and considered it a good day at the office.

For most of the first half the two teams seem evenly matched. Toulouse break through a couple of times, but don't seem able to finish as easily as usual, and you can feel that their confidence is brittle. After half an hour they do score, but at the break they are only 5–0 up and we feel anything could happen. Perhaps they will finally cut loose, or perhaps the slight edge that we have in the scrums and line-outs will pay off.

In the ten minutes after half-time they kick a penalty and score an unconverted try, but we don't let go of the game as we have on other occasions. With 30 minutes to go I come on, and am so excited to finally be back playing that twice I go rushing up in defence with an over-eager, big swinging arm and bounce off tackles.

Eventually, I settle down and start enjoying the game. Our defensive line is swarming over them, and Rickus Lubbe, our South African centre, is having a great game containing Jauzion. I latch on to their number eight as he goes to ground, and get my hands on the ball, but am turned side on as their forwards arrive. My leg is jammed under him at an awkward angle and I get hammered as they try to clear me out. For a moment I think my knee has given way: a bolt of lightning shoots through my leg and the joint bends in a way nature never intended. But as I gingerly get up it seems to be still working and we get the penalty. Over the last 20 minutes we really turn up the heat, until a couple of uncharacteristically bad throw-ins in their half from Olivier Diomandé, who has come on as replacement hooker, put paid to any chance of a win. Still, in the last minute we finally scramble over the line from a tap penalty and need only the conversion to secure a bonus point. But Coco swings it wide, and we have to settle for 13–5.

Afterwards in the changing-room we are almost euphoric, and at the after-match function various Toulouse fans ask us to sign flags and jerseys and programmes, which, if scant reward for the evening's efforts, is a mark of respect and a welcome dose of flattery. I run into Slade McFarland, who has recently arrived as a replacement for the injured William Servat, and was on the bench for Toulouse. The last time I saw him was in 1991, when we were kids playing for the New Zealand Under 19s. He is talking to a sponsor, a man from EADS, the giant multinational behind Airbus, and one of several financial heavyweights that pour money into the rugby club that has the biggest budget in the world. (Ordinarily one or two English clubs may have been able to lay claim to this title, but the salary cap in place in the English championship, even though widely acknowledged as a farce, makes it impossible to get any idea of real figures.)

By this stage of the season there is a yawning gap between the big teams and the little teams. The clubs qualified for Europe, all with budgets over €7.5 million, have between 50 and 62 points and are jostling for position for the semifinals and next year's Heineken Cup qualifications. The minnows like us have only half as much. Along with Narbonne, we are on 25 points, just ahead of Pau on 21 in the red zone of 13th place, while Bayonne, largely thanks to their surprise win over Toulouse, have breathing space on 31. Toulon, the backmarker, are already coming to terms with the fact they will be back down to the second division next year: they have only 12 points. Between the two poles are Brive and Agen on 37 and 43 respectively.

The direct correlation between money and success is hard to miss, although luckily there are one or two anomalies that keep it interesting: Narbonne, who have the smallest budget, €5.8 million, and don't look to have much future in the élite of French rugby in the long term, keep pulling it off against the odds, while Montferrand, at second place on the money table with more than €10 million, are the serial underperformers of the competition.

'Professional sport' is in one sense an oxymoron. A fundamental principle of any sporting contest is that it take place on a level playing-field, but when one side has two, or even three, times as much money as the other the odds are heavily weighted in their favour. The worst of it is that the circle is as virtuous for the 'haves' as it is vicious for the 'have-nots': the more money you have, the more likely you are to be successful, and your success will attract more money still. This can jeopardise interest in the competition: if the outcome of a game is predictable, why bother watching?

The hope of watching David sneak a victory against Goliath still has people coming to watch obvious mismatches, and the home-and-away thing adds a bit of spice in France, but the gap between big and little teams is growing into a gulf, and there is only limited interest in watching Goliath smashing David to a pulp again and again. Since I have been playing in France the first division has shrunk from 24 teams to 14 in an effort to ensure a quality spectacle for the punters, without whom there would be no sponsors, no money and no competition. But the best games are the relatively rare occasions where Goliath is up against Goliath (or, occasionally, David against David).

Rugby is particularly vulnerable to accusations of predictability in terms of results: the rules of the game have been engineered to produce numerous scoring opportunities, and thus high scores, so the better team have more scope to make sure the scoreboard reflects their superiority. The Rugby World Cup is a typical example. It may be difficult to predict the eventual winner, but you know it will be one of a small handful of top teams. In fact, you can fairly accurately predict the semifinalists simply by looking at the draw; with one or two exceptions, pool games are rarely as interesting as their equivalents in the FIFA World Cup.

This is problematic for the future of the sport, and there have been various suggestions as to how to fix it, at least at club level. The salary cap is one option, but the English example seems to show this is not worth the effort. The smaller clubs stick to it simply because they don't have any more money, while the big boys easily circumvent the problem by providing 'jobs' for their players with major sponsors, much the same as during the bad old days of shamateurism. In essence, Joe Blow signs a contract with his club for £50,000, and this is his salary as a club professional. The club is concerned that Joe might want a little more to be going on with, particularly since another club has offered him £60,000, so they have a word with their sponsor, Acme Cleaning Products, who find Joe a particularly well-remunerated position doing next to nothing for £30,000 a year. So Joe is on £80,000, but only £50,000 shows up on the club's books, allowing it to comply with the salary cap.

The same kind of system is already in place in France, where it is referred to as 'image rights': the sponsor may use your photo for marketing purposes, or you may have to attend a corporate bunfight to add a little sporting glamour to the otherwise dull proceedings. This has a double benefit to the club: it avoids the heavy taxes for employees, and ensures the money is not considered part of the *masse salariale*, which is not allowed to be more than 55 percent of a club's overall budget.

This means published figures for club's budgets are not entirely trustworthy. Biarritz, for example, reckon they have a budget of €8.5 million, just €2 million more than Montpellier. I guess it is possible to assemble the sort of all-star team that, like the Real Madrid of Beckham, Zidane and Ronaldo, is nicknamed The Galactics, on just €8.5 million and a love of the Basque country and its climate, but I have my doubts.

Another option is the draft principle along the lines of American football or basketball, where the bottom-placed clubs get first choice at the new talent. This is probably unworkable for several reasons. Players are not yet paid enough that you can oblige them to move from one part of France to another, and clubs would be discouraged from bringing up players through their *centres de formation*, training academies, if they run the risk of losing them at the end. (Currently clubs have to pay a fee to the feeder club if they sign a player out of a *centre de formation*.) And it is notoriously difficult to make the right choices about young players who are yet to be exposed to top-level competition.

One of the things that puzzles me about the people who have been indirectly paying me for the last nine years is why. Why do they do it? What is in it for the sponsors? In the unlikely event that I were ever to become rich enough to be sitting on the sort of money necessary to invest in professional sport, I could think of plenty of other things I would want to spend it on before distributing largesse to a bunch of hairy-arsed schoolboys running around in shorts. Still, there's no getting around the fact that more and more people are pouring money into the game, and they can't all be idiots.

In the spirit of investigative journalism I go along to one of the sponsors' monthly lunch parties in Montpellier, and find there are a number of different reasons, depending on the size of the business and the money it can put into the club. At the lower end of the scale are businesses that simply buy season tickets, which allow them to come to games and have access to after-match receptions. Montpellier suffers from having a stadium well past its use-by date so there are no corporate boxes, but the club has cunningly decided to spend a lot of money on excellent food and drink. If sponsors come for the rugby, they stay on late for the *foie gras* and other delicacies served by the Brasserie du Corum, washed down by unlimited quantities of wine and beer in a party atmosphere. Often the businesses are relatively small and the owners simply enjoy going to the rugby and having a knees-up afterwards, and they can take along a client or whomever they feel like and slip the season tickets into the communications budget, thereby making the whole thing tax-deductible.

Bigger outfits are happy enough with the rugby and the party, but they also come for the schmoozing. Rugby's egalitarian atmosphere means potential clients can be met in an informal setting and useful alliances made while discussing whether Montpellier should have kicked for goal, or taken the scrum, or the referee who has it in for us, or indeed anything from the vast panoply of rubbish that people talk about after a game. 'Jobs for the boys' is a common theme in business all around the world, but perhaps even more so in France, where cultivating *le piston*—the contact—is an art form. Here in Montpellier, the Agglomeration is the major sponsor, and they are also responsible for spending a massive envelope of taxpayers' money on roadworks and building projects, so rubbing shoulders with the people from the Agglomeration can be well worth your while if you can provide anything they might want to buy.

The really *big* sponsors—the ones who put hundreds of thousands, or even millions, of euros into the clubs every season—have a variety of reasons for spending on rugby. For *les mécènes*, the corporate philanthropists, it seems to be a hobby that doubles as a useful marketing ploy. Serge Kampf bankrolls Biarritz and the French Barbarians. Pierre Fabre at Castres, Max Guazzini at Stade Français and the Michelin family at Montferrand are all multimillionaires in their own right, and can afford to dabble in a sport that has high media exposure without being as expensive as football. They probably consider the emotional return on their monetary investment justification in itself. This is not to say they are simply rich dilettantes—I suspect you don't get to the top of the pile by splurging on a whim—but they are not particularly concerned to get a concrete return on their investment.

This is not the case for Orange, the France Telecom Group, which sponsors a number of rugby teams, as well as football teams, and must justify their spending. Working out how much the space on the front of a jersey is worth must be a hell of a job, and quantifying the returns on sponsors' money far from simple. There are people who are paid to note the amount of screen-time a particular sponsor's logo gets. How much attention viewers pay to a logo, consciously or unconsciously, while watching a game must be almost impossible to gauge, and what it is worth compared to an equivalent amount spent on conventional advertising is anybody's guess.

Then there are the *collectivités*—the towns or regions who spend taxpayers' money on professional sports teams because they consider sport a drawcard and see the team as standard-bearers for the town. In Montpellier the prime mover behind the massive taxpayer funding of the rugby club is the former mayor and current head of the Agglomeration and the Languedoc-Roussillon region, Georges Frêche. Something of a benevolent dictator, Frêche has said that the rugby he played as a young man taught him important values, and he wants to encourage the youth of Montpellier to learn the same thing. He clearly feels that the best way of promoting the game in the region is by implanting Montpellier in the élite of French rugby. Not only has the Agglomeration been paying the lion's share of the club's budget, it has also stumped up most of the €60 million for the construction of the new stadium. While this has obviously been of massive benefit to the club, allowing it to make giant strides over the last five years, having most of your money dependent on political goodwill is a precarious state of affairs. Frêche is coming to the end of his tenure, and there is no guarantee his successor will be as enamoured of the oval-ball game.

The danger of finding a black hole in the middle of your budget is very real in French rugby. Over the nine years I have been playing in the country, four clubs have been relegated for financial reasons, and every year there is talk of money trouble dogging one or more of the élite clubs. Toulon, Grenoble, Colomiers and Bègles-Bordeaux have all paid the price for miscalculating what was coming in and what was going out. When this happens it leaves the club in ruins. Players depart *en masse*, and new management comes in to pick up the pieces. The road back is not an easy one. This year, Toulon made it up to the first division after five years in the second division, only to discover that this time round they were too cautious with their money, and by not investing in the necessary talent they didn't have the fire-power to compete at the top level.

There is every chance that this will continue to be a common theme in the coming years. As the gulf between first and second divisions becomes unbridgeable, there will be a yo-yo system of clubs coming up, getting hammered for a year *à la* Toulon, then going straight back down. Lyon look like being the one club that might be able to put together the kind of long-term project necessary to survive in the top flight, largely because they are a major city and benefit from the kind of heavyweight financial backing that is unavailable to smaller clubs—unless a moneybags turns up and decides to throw money at it until the required results arrive. And even then, money on its own is no guarantee of success: it needs to be intelligently spent, which is not always as straightforward as it sounds.

Winter Blues

Every year, Montpellier seem to go through a lean period over the winter months from November to March, and this year has been no exception. But unlike other years where, if there has been cause for concern, it has never been more than superficial, this time the cracks run deep. The reason seems to be twofold. Unlike previous years, where we set ourselves the limited goal of avoiding relegation, this year we have set our sights higher—between sixth and eighth place—so the fact we are still languishing near the bottom in twelfth means that, by our own standards, we are underperforming. This, together with an influx of new players impatient with a structure that doesn't seem to be working, has led to a widespread questioning of the system in place.

Over the last couple of years, the move from second-division semi-professionals to first-division professionals has cut a swathe through the ranks of Montpellier's old guard. Of the squad of 33 who won the second-division championship, only ten are left. As semi-professionals, tied to Montpellier by links other than rugby and feeling implicated in the future of the club—and therefore less likely to rock the boat than the 'mercenaries' like me who have replaced them—they became victims of their own success. If Montpellier had stayed in second division, most of them would still be playing for the club.

Of the twenty-three who no longer play for the club, only four retired. Two became assistant coaches: the talented Catalan centre Pat Arlettaz, who runs the backs, and Didier Bes, the former hooker and captain, who resembles an amiable garden gnome on steroids, and is in charge of the forwards. Both play an important role, not only as coaches but also as surrogate group leaders.

The clear-out of old players has left a vacuum at the heart of the group, and although the captain, Jérôme Vallée, himself a survivor of the old team, is a good player and a good bloke he lacks the stature to pull everyone together. He seems to want a democracy-style chat-fest where every player has a say, but when the inevitable happens and everybody starts talking at once he blows up. This affects his own performance and he often reacts badly to pressure, trying to take on all the responsibilities of running the team—calling line-outs, making tactical decisions—when he is not the best qualified for the job. His status is not helped by the lingering suspicion that he was appointed captain because he is such a genuinely hard worker and nice guy he would be unlikely to question the authority of the coach. Recently, as the rumblings of discontent have grown louder, this has started to change and he has been forced into confrontation with Nourault.

During the course of a season, the leaders, and the underlying attitude of the group itself, may change for a variety of reasons. Leaders may be injured or dropped, lessening their legitimacy in the eyes of everyone else. New arrivals may assert themselves, forming a new hub of power as different individuals form alliances to make up new sub-groups. If this is starting to resemble a David Attenborough documentary on silverback gorillas, it is fair to say that there are a number of similarities—apart from the obvious physical ones. The group is a complex and interesting structure, relatively impenetrable to an outsider, that has no obvious hierarchy apart from the captain and the coach, and both these positions are unstable, particularly in clubs performing below par.

The single most important part of any squad is the coach. He answers to the club president, who hired him and will almost certainly eventually fire him, but while in place he calls the shots. He is responsible for recruiting players, training them, and picking the team to play on the day. A good coach should have good managerial skills; good communication skills—listening to what his players think, as well as telling them what to do; an ability to motivate different individuals in different ways; and be someone the players feel they can trust, and for whom they want to play well: ideally, a sort of father figure. He must know the game well enough to be able to analyse problem areas in the performance of individuals and the team, and be able to coach both specific and general skills. And he should have a vision for the team that he can impart to them. He needs to have an eye for talent and an ability to plan for the future, and he should be prepared to innovate. Given the demands that will be made on his time, the need for a good work ethic goes without saying. Running a professional outfit has become too much for any one man, so he must also know how to delegate.

The problem is that this is a hell of a lot to ask of anyone; there will always be a gap between the ideal and the reality. In my experience, French coaches suffer from a desire to run everything themselves. One of the problems of the professional generation is this tendency towards shrinking the traditionally generous spirit of rugby. The importance of the team used to be paramount, whereas now power-sharing is seen as a kind of weakness, or at the very least a loss of control. Coaches want to centralise decision-making because they know it's their head on the block, and understandably they prefer to make their own mistakes, rather than be fired for someone else's. This makes for a strange relationship between the coach and his players. Although he's in charge, everyone knows that he is the one more likely to pay for poor performance, simply because it is easier to fire one man than thirty. Hence the players retain a certain power over him.

It is difficult to say whether France is exceptional in this way, but the revolutionary culture is still alive and well in its rugby teams. Over nine years I have had four different coaches. One—former French coach Jacques Fouroux—was fired during the season. One—Saïsset—almost went while I was there but then went a short time afterwards, despite taking the team to a European Cup final and, the following year, to the final of the French championship; he was given notice the day after the final. And my current coach, Didier Nourault, looks increasingly unlikely to survive the growing clamour for his head. In every case, the impetus came from the players.

A relationship with the coach is tricky to handle. I try to have a close dialogue so I get regular feedback about how he sees my game, and I can tell him what I think about the training sessions and how the team is shaping up. Perhaps because I'm older—closer in age to the coach than to some of the younger players in the team—I look for the kind of relationship you might have with a colleague. As a rule, though, players tend to see the coach as a boss-teacher hybrid. This means the relationship quite often spills into a conflict situation, us against him.

What I see as my adult, open-dialogue style of doing things does leave me open to accusations of arse-kissing, and until I was recently disinherited I was known as being one of Nourault's three or four 'sons'. But at least you know where you are—or you think you do until things go pear-shaped, which they invariably do at some point. When this happens, I tend to fall back on the age-old tradition of spoilt children who stick out their bottom lip and pout: I stomp around in a black cloud of ill-humour until I get back in the team. Not pretty, I know, but it does seem to be effective. It's not the sort of thing you could get away with in England or New Zealand, where your lip is supposed to remain stoically firm come what may, but the French seem more ready to accept the temperamental shenanigans of their men.

The mercurial nature of the French means the psychological aspect of the team is extraordinarily important. I still find it astonishing that the same team can play so well one weekend and cravenly badly the following, for no apparent reason. Although it's the fault of individual players, the onus falls on the coach to come up with some form of social engineering that will lead the team to fulfil its potential. So every year we have team-building exercises. I have rock-climbed, abseiled, bungy-jumped, canoed, mountain-biked and done community work, all in the name of team-building. I count myself lucky. Other teams have been on military camps, overland treks and one year, at the end of a long day's march, the players from one team were given live chickens, a knife and a box of matches and told to sort dinner out for themselves.

The jury is out on how useful these things are. A couple of years ago Montferrand were taken on a gruelling week-long trek through the Massif Central, bivouacking wherever they could. Their coach, Alain Hyardet, said it was a great success and he now knew whom he could count on in the team as the difficult conditions had brought out the best in certain people. He was, he announced, going to construct his group around these guys, whom he saw as the real leaders.

This sounds like bollocks. If you were to give me a compass and map and send me off into the great outdoors with a handful of unfortunate team-mates under orders to follow me, I could virtually guarantee we would be hopelessly lost and shivering in a ditch with hypothermia within twenty-four hours. But why would this exclude me from a leadership role on a rugby field? All it would show is that I'm hopeless at hiking.

Anyway in February, as the team looks like it is starting to unravel, Nourault decides we need a bit of team-building. This is unusual because it is the sort of exercise usually done during pre-season training, but he is canny enough to know that he is losing his grip on proceedings, and his only hope is that the team will start to grow up and take more responsibility for itself. The plan is to divide us into five crews who will race catamarans on the Mediterranean (with the help, mercifully, of qualified skippers), interspersed with three hour-long sessions with a sports psychologist, and some fitness training.

None of this sounds unreasonable. We start off with a serious-minded regatta before lunch and everyone plays along, steering or grinding or whatever, according to their designated role, and we agree it is good fun, although it is bitterly cold on the water despite the winter sun. But the boys have figured out there isn't actually much to do—the skippers are capable of sailing the boats more or less on their own— so it is suggested a few drinks may keep out the cold when we go back on the water that evening. In the interval between dinner and the session with the shrink, stocks are laid in for the night.

The sports psychologist is a vast improvement on the previous year, when we had to suffer the New Age idiocy of some pony-tailed, leather-trousered charlatan and his mishmash of eastern religions, power crystals and coloured lights. This year the psychologist is a young woman and not unattractive. She goes over what is well-trodden ground for most of us—mental imagery, relaxation techniques, and so on.

Concentration levels are not high, and the hour sprawls into an hour and a half as her role devolves into one of crowd control over a bunch of catcalling kindergarten children. Afterwards we have an exhausting fitness session, then more psychology before dinner. By this point some of the lads are lying on the floor asleep, and the poor woman can't get her video to work, and she asks if anyone can show the team how to do the haka, which she considers the pinnacle of pre-match preparation. I am reluctant, but I can't help feeling sorry for her and am about to oblige when Harley Crane, a fellow Kiwi, points out that it wouldn't be right. Like all New Zealanders, we consider the haka special, sacred even, not the kind of fairground attraction that should be performed for a laugh, and certainly not something to be shared with Frenchies, who would tend to take the piss out of it.

After dinner we are back on the boats, supposedly to go racing until three or four in the morning, although the clanking of bottles in the overnight bags hint at what the team has designated as its real priority. The coach has arranged a midnight snack a few miles down the coast before we turn and head for home, but by the time we're halfway there all the boys are munted, having played drinking games, sung songs, and shouted insults at each other over the boat's radio. Fake 'man overboard' calls, cancellations of the 'race'—to which only the skippers are now paying any attention—national anthems, dirty jokes: everything comes washing over the radio.

When our skipper thinks he may have a problem—something is bumping against the hull of the €650,000 boat for which he is responsible—he tries to get in touch with the safety boat carrying the organisers so they can come and have a look. However, he is shouted down by a chorus of hoaxers. 'Jean-Pierre here. You seem to be being attacked by a ten-metre shark, WATCH OUT! FOR GOD'S SAKE, WATCH OUT! AAARRGGGHHH...' 'Okay, we're sending in the scuba team. Standby for Operation Rainbow Warrior. I repeat, standby for Operation Rainbow Warrior.'

Any attempt to suggest the situation is serious just leads to an increase in volume. When we arrive at the rendezvous point, the crews reel in and quickly start throwing food around. A couple of senior players mash cheese into each other's hair. Other players urinate into the marina. And watching over the whole thing with a sickly smile, because he doesn't know quite how to rein in the chaos he has unwittingly unleashed, is Nourault.

We would never have got this out of hand at the start of the year. Last year Nourault roared with fury when he saw Olivier Diomandé, our Muslim hooker, eating chips he had been given by the well-intentioned but not very nutrition-minded catering staff because he couldn't eat a side order of peas that had been sprinkled with bacon. The general feeling was that this sort of thing was a bit much, but everyone kept their heads down. However, Nourault's credibility has waned over the last few months, and rather than supporting him we have made an unspoken decision to cut him adrift. He can feel it, and knows he no longer has the authority to lay down the law. When we stagger into breakfast the next morning, he is genuinely solicitous: 'Everyone sleep all right? Not too tired?'

The final hour of psychology passes smoothly enough because everyone is too knackered to backchat. As we shamble off home, I can't help thinking the whole thing has been a complete waste of time, but the following weekend we play probably our best game of the season to date, so the management consider the expedition an unqualified success.

Perhaps they're right. If pushed, I would say that recreational team-drinking is a good thing: it provides the social lubricant that helps work relationships become friendships, and the better you get on with people the more likely you are to play well with them. There was also an element of group muscle-flexing that was no doubt beneficial. Fighting for your right to party is not exactly textbook mental preparation for professional athletes, but if you're all in it together maybe it doesn't matter what you do.

Each team forms its own sense of identity around a hard core of a few influential players, who tend to have formed tight bonds to the club itself over, if not a career, at least a few years. They are the temple guardians, experienced, charismatic players who set the tone for the approach to the season. Players who arrive from elsewhere try to fit in with the way things are done because it is the basis of the team's *esprit de corps*, and, although it might not be what you're used to, no one wants to look as though they're being difficult, and adapting is part of the life of the professional player.

Here in Montpellier, for example, the backs—known disconcertingly as 'The Sect'—have their own monthly meeting over dinner. Among other things they discuss the state of the team, and vote on their choice for 'zero of the month', generally a forward. It is supposed to be a secret affair, and the minutes are solemnly noted down. From time to time, some of the forwards try to find out where the meeting is so they can steal the minutes, or spray shaving foam on the backs' cars. If this sounds futile and childish, you have to remember that we are grown men being paid to run around in shorts after an inflated pigskin. Our whole existence reeks of childishness and futility. And this kind of thing has the merit of bringing players together in a relaxed atmosphere away from the eyes and ears of the coaching staff. And it is a tradition, which is important for such a young club.

New players, however, will subscribe to a system only as long as it seems to be working. There is too much at stake for the mercenary to sit back and go with the flow when the flow looks like it is leading up you up a certain creek without the proverbial paddle. The club has brought in experienced players who are highly conscious of the stain that a drop into the second division would represent on their curriculum vitae.

As the grumbling gets louder, people move from quibbling about the direction the ship should be taking to calling their agent and trying to make sure there is a place for them in a lifeboat somewhere. Once this happens, things can quickly go wrong. The mercenary has a limited stake in the future of a club; what is of paramount importance to him is that he looks good enough to get a decent contract next time the meat market opens. This sounds ugly and to some extent it is, but it comes to this only when a player feels he has exhausted all his options.

Initially, a player pours his guts into a new club. You want to believe it can work, and that you have value to add. But if by March things are shaping up badly, looking after number one becomes your first priority. Top-flight players with long-term contracts at successful clubs are less likely to find themselves in this position, but for the journeyman plying his trade in the clubs inhabiting the lower regions of the competition it can be an annual event.

The self-centred, short-term focus of the mercenary can exacerbate an already difficult situation. Whispering campaigns blaming captains, coaches, players—basically anyone in range—can lead to a vicious circle of resentment. It is late February as I write this, and I already suspect one or two of my team-mates of looking to the lifeboats, a bad sign. It doesn't really apply to me any more. Given that I am coming to the end of my contract, I won't be going anywhere and am pretty sure I will be retiring—although I change my mind about that weekly.

By now you may have a dark view of the hired rugby player, and it is true that I have not been painting a pretty picture. But I should point out that when I look around the changing-room I can't see a single player whom I think of as lacking in honour or courage, or any of the other noble qualities rugby demands of its players. Certainly the 'pride in the jersey' formula is a little hollow these days, when it is not unusual for a player to represent four or five different teams in the course of his professional career. But that does not mean the core values of self-sacrifice, shared responsibility and team spirit have been jettisoned: it now comes down to self-respect—pride in what you do and how you do it. Being able to look at yourself in the mirror is perhaps more of a guideline than having pride in your team's colours, simply because as a new-comer you can't possibly draw on all the history of a club within the first weeks or months of arriving. But as a rugby player you know about the spirit of rugby; even if you occa-sionally lose sight of things because you're worried about a potential dent in your pay cheque, you still know that the best way of getting something out of rugby—money, pride or whatever—is by putting into it everything you have.

For us, the important thing in these shaky times is that the group's leaders keep the faith and make sure we stay positive. For the two years I have been here these leaders have stayed largely the same: Olivier Diomandé, our hooker from the Ivory Coast, a tireless workhorse who has stayed loyal to the club despite interesting propositions from other clubs; Michel Macurdy, a lock who has occasionally been converted to number eight this season, and is probably our most intelligent reader of the game; Jérôme Vallée, who is growing into the captaincy; 'Bubu'—Sebastian Buada—our ballsy little half-back, an instinctive player rather than a tactician, who gives it everything; Alessandro Stoica, our Italian centre, always well kitted out in designer clothes, sunglasses and fast cars; and the very experienced winger Laurent Arbo, top try-scorer in the history of the French first division.

I am a backbencher, yapping when I feel like it, but deftly sidestepping anything that looks like having heavy responsibility attached: I was captain of Racing Club the year we went down and it was no fun at all. Coco Aucagne should also be in this list of leaders, given that he plays in the key fly-half position and is the only man in the team who has played for France. However, he is so modest he doesn't seem to want to put himself forward, which is a shame because he has much to offer, and we need someone capable of taking proceedings on the field by the scruff of the neck.

All these men have a place in the starting line-up as of right, something else that has been causing tensions. There are no real stars at Montpellier so no one is irreplaceable, and the large number of games that have to be played, plus the fact all 30-odd of the squad are at a similar level, would point towards a policy of rotating players. But too many guys feel they are not being given their chance. This sort of thing happens all the time, but if the team is winning you just shut up and take it. When it is underperforming and you're still not getting a chance, you get irascible.

Worse still, if you're really not playing at all, you have to go down and spend some time in the *Espoirs*. There are some very good young players in the *Espoirs*, mixed in with a few who will never make it to the first division, and the games can be of a reasonable standard. And at least you don't feel the constant pressure to perform.

But really it is a living death for established players—a taste of the anonymity and ordinariness to which you will return after your time in front of the crowd. It is difficult to play well because the team patterns and lines of running are very different to what you are used to. Even if you do play well, it is only what is expected of you. And if you play badly—because you haven't been able to motivate yourself to get involved in what is typically a scrappy affair in front of a couple of people who happen to be passing by, on a potholed, muddy field that looks as though it has been used to grow potatoes, and run by a referee who seems to have no more than a passing acquaintance with the rule book—then you look and feel like a fraud.

The one moment of the week when you can try to stake a claim on your rightful place in the first team comes during the contact sessions, when the As are pitted against the Bs— or, as the English-speaking members of the team call it, the Attack of the Killer Bs. This is when the first team are recovering from the weekend's game, and thinking about the coming weekend, and are really not interested in the rough-and-tumble of full-blooded opposition. After all, they have nothing to prove: they're already where they want to be.

The Killer Bs, on the other hand, have all the motivation in the world, and aren't about to let slip their chance. Even though I think of these sessions as ridiculous, unnecessary and of little use to the first team, if I am stuck in the Killer Bs I, like everyone else, fly into the session with as much determination as I would on a Saturday game, and the end result is that these little half-hour sessions are often won by the B team.

Tensions can run high during these sessions, and at the end of one I find myself, not entirely blamelessly, in a scuffle with Mika Bert, a lock who has been being groomed for the big time and now, aged 26, has broken through and is playing some excellent rugby. Regrettably, this means that he has taken up one of the spots that used to have my name on it, and as I had been doing some of the grooming I am a little put out by his bad manners. To make things right, we have to perform the little ritual of *le bisous de l'amitié*, two henpecks on the cheek. This is the flipside of a French habit that I usually enjoy as it permits you to kiss fragrant, attractive young French women whom you've only just met. Sweaty, unshaven second-rowers whom you've been handbagging a minute before are less agreeable, although the ritual does oblige you to be more sincere than the usual handshake and cursory nod.

Countdown

André Lestorte is no longer president of Pau, and I don't hold any grudges against the team itself, but by the time our return game against them comes around it looks as if the dreaded thirteenth place is reserved for either us or them, and I'd sooner it was them. There are still just a handful of points separating us—they are on 21, while we are on 25. It is now mid March, just ten weeks before the end of the season, and a loss would put us in a very uncomfortable position.

We dominate proceedings and score a couple of good tries, including a peach of an effort from our talented fullback, David Bortolussi, who runs in a chip-and-chase from inside our own half. Again, Beauxis is kicking goals from everywhere and he keeps them in touch, so we go to the break leading 20–12.

It is difficult not to think that the whole thing is running according to script and with luck we'll manage a bonus point for four tries. But all the hard work of the first spell is undone within ten minutes of the start of the second. A converted try and a penalty and we are staring the unthinkable in the face—Pau are beating us 22–20 at home with just half an hour to go. Knowing this game is do-or-die for both teams, busloads of their supporters have turned up, and the Montpellier crowd, never particularly vocal, is being swamped by chants of 'Sec-tion!' Clap-clap-clap. 'Sec-tion!' and Pau's green and white flags are waving furiously. We reserves—I am on the bench again—have been buggering about, thinking we don't have any worries, but suddenly everyone is tense, gnawing at fingernails, tut-tutting at the referee and swearing softly to each other. With just under half an hour to go, I am relieved to get on the field. Out in the middle you have less time to think about the consequences; you just slip into doing what you know.

Pau aren't creating anything, they are just living off our mistakes, so we tighten up the game and go back to rolling mauls, forcing a penalty, which Coco kicks, and then we drive over in the corner from a line-out, and from the restart we head up field again. Pau are panicking now, giving away silly penalties as they feel the game sliding away from them, and Christophe Laussucq, their halfback, cracks and punches our prop, Clément Baiocco. The referee doesn't see it but the touch judge does, and Coco puts the penalty over again: 31–22.

Now that their team is losing, Pau's backs, realising they have to take chances, start to operate with more menace. They run back a sloppy missed touch-finder from inside their half, and a well-timed grubber kick is gathered by Cassin, who scores. Beauxis converts. 31–29. Christ. Twenty minutes to go. At least the crowd are getting their money's worth. Play see-saws back and forth, each side kicking long and hoping the other will make a mistake.

Ten minutes to go. Seb Kuzbik, our big powerful winger, breaks down the left flank and scores, and Coco converts. That's the bonus point and surely the game. As Kuzbik was sliding in to touch down, one of Pau's defenders had come across and spitefully dropped his knees into his back, so the referee awards us a penalty on the halfway line. Once Coco has converted the try he slots this one as well: 41–29.

Pau are not finished yet, and after we take the kick-off Bubu sets himself up for a kick that will relieve the pressure. Patrick Tabacco, Pau's tall back-rower, leaps to charge it down. The ball bounces kindly into his arms and he is away, beating our cover defence to score his second try. Beauxis converts, and with the score at 41–36 we spend a nervous last couple of minutes down in their end before the final whistle releases us from purgatory. Pau come away with a bonus point but so do we, and with the four points for a win that should be enough.

A week later, I am again in the starting line-up for the return match against Brive. In fact, I'm starting to feel pretty good, and am thinking more and more seriously about playing another season. The day before the game I am interviewed in the local paper and asked if I am retiring. I leave the door ajar, replying that I am 95 percent certain this will be my last year. When you're enjoying playing rugby, winning games, having fun with your mates and the money is piling up nicely in the bank, you can't think of a better job. What's so good about the real world anyway?

Things start to go wrong pretty much as soon as these thoughts form. That night the neighbours decide to have a party, and one of the guests accompanies the Gipsy Kings on the bongos until three in the morning. It doesn't get much worse. I am a bit grumpy the next day, but after all it's the best job in the world, so let's get on with it. Then it does get worse: I hear a rumour that Samuel Chinarro, a Brive lock, is in contact with Montpellier about next year. As I am the only lock without a contract for next year, it's my spot he would be taking. Still, there's probably nothing in it. Idle chit-chat. Happens all the time. Agents trying to talk up the value of their player, that sort of thing. As I say, let's get on with it.

We start well, and I get the impression Brive are not very interested—they're in ninth position on 38 points, well out of the danger zone. Pau are still thirteenth on 24, while we're eleventh on 30. Agen, in eighth place, are on 48, ten points ahead of Brive, and then it's another four or five points to the European clubs—realistically, an unbridgeable gap. So Brive haven't much to play for. After four minutes it's 3–0 to us. Here we go…

Then we make a couple of mistakes and they kick a penalty to touch 15 metres out. No danger there though: we defend well, particularly at home. Famous last words: they get a clean take and the most ordinary-looking maul spins off—helped by my incompetence as I try to pull them apart but succeed only in splintering our defence—and Chinarro, the would-be Montpellier lock, plunges into the in-goal to score.

Sweet mercy, what have I done to deserve this? After ten minutes it's 7–3 to them. We really need to win this game because our last few matches are against heavyweights, apart from Toulon whom we play at home, and if we're not careful we will be scratching around in the basement again, despite having worked so hard to get out. We bounce back quickly with a penalty, and then Murphy Taele crashes it up in midfield after a scrum. I come in to clean out, and collect his boot in my face as he's wiggling around on the ground with his feet in the air, like a dying insect.

Bubu picks up the ball and darts 20 metres through their non-existent defence to touch down, but I don't see any of this because I am looking at the blood on my hand that seems to be coming out of my eye. Surely not. This is ridiculous. Oh well, at least we're winning now. I go off to have my injury looked at. It will need a stitch but isn't as bad as it might have been.

I get back on just after Coco kicks another penalty and we are starting to look reasonably comfortable. I find the rhythm easy, and after the initial panic I relax and start to enjoy it. Both teams are trying to play an open game and we are often a little too ambitious, attempting miracle passes that don't connect. Brive kick another two penalties, Coco drops a goal, and at half-time it's 19–13. We dominate without managing to score, and with 30 minutes to go I am hauled off. Shortly afterwards, Brive's young lock, Denys Drozdz, gets a yellow card and we strike almost immediately: a try for Seb Kuzbik. That wraps it up, 24–13, with neither side able to score in a strangely flat last 25 minutes.

The return match against Clermont-Ferrand, scheduled for the end of January, had to be put off because of flooding, and we finally play it at the end of March. The delay is a blessing: by this time the atmosphere in the team has changed considerably for the better. We have managed to string together a few wins, and a conscious effort has been made to bind the group together. A system of fines has been instituted for people who arrive late at training or team meetings, have their photograph in the paper, or allow their cellphone to ring in team meetings. If a ball is dropped during a team run, everyone does ten press-ups. And after home games the team gets together in the changing-room, has a few beers, and nominates contenders for the 'wig of the week' award. Anyone guilty of a cock-up has to wear a long blond wig at the after-match function and to and from training sessions during the week. If this seems contrived, it is nonetheless effective, and gives everyone the opportunity to have a laugh and let off some steam while atoning for various sins, real or imagined.

I come off the bench at half-time, when the score is 15–10 to us. Our backs played well and after only 15 minutes we were 15–0 up, but just before half-time the Springbok winger Breyton Paulse got a bit of room on the short side and sprinted 60 metres for a try that could destabilise everything we have painstakingly put together. Shortly after the break,

Laurent Arbo scores from broken play and all the steam goes out of Montferrand. Having hoped for a semifinal berth, they are now looking to hang on to sixth place to assure themselves of qualifying for the European Cup next year, so they have plenty to play for, but they seem to go to pieces.

Aurélien Rougerie, the French winger and their usual captain, is out injured so that may have something to do with it, but given their talent and experience—Argentinian, Italian and French internationals sprinkled through the team, along with former All Black flanker Sam Broomhall, Welsh Lion Stephen Jones at fly-half, Paulse on the wing and so on—it is little short of a disgrace. Admittedly, Canadian Jamie Cudmore gets an ill-deserved red card with 15 minutes to go, but by the end the only people who seem to be trying are Tony Marsh, the Kiwi who played in the French midfield for a few years up to 2003, and Jones, who is leaving at the end of the season to go back to Llanelli. That may be a little unfair on some of them—God knows I've slogged my guts out in losing teams often enough—but the end result is a stunning 42–13 landslide. We score five tries, the fourth one when we atomise their scrum (a man down without Cudmore) five metres out from the line on their put-in, thus collecting a bonus point.

I have a word with Tony Marsh afterwards, and ask him what is going on. He tells me it's the same story they've had at Montferrand for the last six years. Over that time they've changed the coach four times. The team never has time to settle into a pattern, and I suspect their policy of buying stars doesn't help, because all stars tend to think of themselves as individuals, and naturally want to keep the habits that have allowed them to become successful. The French have a culinary image for the idea that different elements may come together to form a successful whole: *Est-ce que la mayonnaise va prendre?* Montferrand's experience shows that even the best quality ingredients don't help if the chef doesn't know how to make mayonnaise, or doesn't have the time. I also talk to Jamie Cudmore, who tells me that life for Montferrand is, in fact, too easy. Everything is on a plate, nothing has to be fought for—there are no contact sessions with the Killer Bs, for example—and it is easy to get soft in such a cosy environment.

My Beautiful Career

After the Montferrand game, we have a weekend off while the semifinals of the European Cup are played. We take advantage of this to play the annual foreigners' cricket match organised by former Sydneysider Anthony Hill in Narbonne. Anthony is a year younger than I am but he wrecked his back last year playing for Montpellier and was forced into retirement. He now owns and runs a bar in Narbonne. Take one Australian former rugby player, give him unlimited access to beer, and a slipped disc that means he can't exercise, and nature inevitably takes its course: this former professional athlete now sports a silhouette to rival Homer Simpson. But he does have his uses, and cricket day is worth circling in your diary.

We are told to arrive at ten-thirty in the morning, but when we get there well after eleven people are still dribbling in. What French rugby journalists refer to as 'the Foreign Legion' looks more like a shambling mob of irregulars after a night on the booze. Some of the boys have managed to find one-day cricket outfits in the appropriate colours, and Dwayne Haare, who seemed quite keen on taking my head off last time I saw him, is wearing a wig to go with his beige slacks, and a mud-coloured shirt that is obviously a tribute to the Kiwi one-day teams of the 1980s and '90s.

Anthony manages to pry us away from the bar about one o'clock and we head out to convert a local rugby field into the hallowed turf of the Melbourne Cricket Ground or the Basin Reserve, or whatever you fancy. As there are more New Zealanders than any other nationality, it is decided the contest is New Zealand v. The Rest of the World. I am startled to find myself opening the batting, and even more startled when I remember how hard that little red cricket ball is, and see the speed at which South African Breyton Paulse is chucking the thing down. I had boosted my confidence with a few pre-match drinks, but I feel it slipping away as I realise that I forgot to put a box in and, aided by an unpredictable pitch, the ball is zipping around and my bat is not always where it ought to be. Mercifully, the ordeal is soon over and I can head back to the bar. The rest of the day is a blur. For the record, New Zealand won but it was close.

Our return match against Narbonne comes a couple of weeks later, and there is a little more riding on the outcome. Still, there doesn't seem to be much pressure. We are still in twelfth place but there is now an eight-point gap between us and Pau, while Brive, Bayonne and Narbonne are four points, two points and one point ahead respectively. We haven't won an away game yet, and this is probably our last chance. I am on the bench. The reserves have arranged a sweepstake for the first player to get on—€10 each in the pot, €70 for the winner—so there is more than usual enthusiasm about stretching and warming up in case Nourault looks over.

We start well, recovering our own kick-off, and before a minute is up Coco slots a drop goal and we are up 3–0. Then he misses a couple of penalties he would normally put over. He gets the next one though—6–0—and we are dominating them in the scrum to such an extent it should be the platform for a comfortable victory. Jason Hooper, who anchored the Kiwi batting line-up with the kind of raw but efficient agricultural style that you would expect from a prop, gets yellow-carded this time, and once again Coco does the honours.

It's now 9–0 and Narbonne are struggling. However, we seem to be going for miracle passes that don't quite go to hand and don't manage to develop an insurmountable lead. Cédric Rosalen, Narbonne's kicker, misses a penalty attempt and then makes up for it just before half-time, so as we go to the break they are still in touch.

In the second half, Narbonne get their act together quickly. A well-worked try by Lionel Mazars and another Rosalen penalty to go with the conversion mean that after quarter of an hour they have the lead and momentum: 9–3 has become 9–13. A minute later their fullback, Nicolas Nadau, attempts a drop goal from the halfway line. It's so far out it looks impossible, but the ball sails between the posts. 9–16.

By now I am bouncing around on the sideline like a jack-in-the-box, trying to catch Nourault's eye and get on to claim the €70. Saving the day would be nice as well. Montpellier finally react and start exerting a bit of pressure, but Coco misses another penalty. David Bortolussi goes off the bench to pick up the €70 and a few minutes later is handed the kicking duties. This time it goes over: 12–16. Five minutes later he does it again: 15–16.

Ten minutes to go and things are getting interesting. Neither side seems to have a knockout punch, but Rosalen kicks a penalty to make it that much farther for us to go: 15–19. Five minutes left and we have to score a try or kick two penalties to win. With a couple of minutes on the clock we are awarded a penalty about 20 yards out. If we go for the posts we will still be a point short, and they will kick-off deep to us and let the clock run down, so we elect to kick for touch and hope to drive over from a line-out about five metres out.

Unfortunately we cock it up and they clear to touch. There are still a few seconds to run and we have possession. We launch a final attack, lining up our giant Samoan prop Philemon Toleafoa in the hope that he will go rampaging through to the line. But the move is telegraphed and there are already four guys in orange and black ready to leap in front of the juggernaut. Phil can see them coming and is already trying to calculate the best angle to run. While he is doing this he takes his eye off the ball, and when it arrives he spills it. The final whistle blows. We get a bonus point, but again it could have—should have—been more.

After the game, I bail up Nourault and say I hope the reason he didn't use me was that he wanted to keep me fresh for the game against Toulon. He says they haven't yet decided who will play in that game, but Sam Nouchi will certainly be starting, and I will be starting in the game after that because it is against Perpignan. This means I will almost certainly not even be on the bench for the Toulon game. Before Perpignan, I won't have played for the best part of a month.

I try to bluff Nourault by saying that I don't want to look like a fool against my old club, and I'd rather not start if he doesn't give me a chance against Toulon. Some hope. He calls my bluff: I don't play against Toulon, and when Perpignan rolls around I'm warming the bench again. Worse still, the two games after that are Agen and Biarritz, and Sam used to play for both these clubs.

After my injury in Toulon, the club recruited Drickus Hancke from South Africa and he has proved to be an excellent player, younger and more dynamic than me and a good workhorse. He is now first choice for the five jersey, so Sam and I scrap over who gets to sit on the bench. Drickus is a good guy and we have become great friends, so I can't resent him his success. He has adapted well to the team, something Alex Codling never managed because he spent too much time making comparisons between his experiences in British rugby and the way things are done in France: inevitably these comparisons were unfavourable to Montpellier. To give Alex his due, he wasn't necessarily wrong, and his bad back injury wouldn't have helped his mood, but he was so negative the other players cut him adrift, rather than helping him integrate. This weighed on him as well, and he ended up in a difficult position.

Current club gossip revolves around who is doing what

next year. As things have been better for a while and we look relatively safe from relegation, most of the team look like staying, although a few have been entertaining offers from other clubs. Clement and Dio have received serious offers from Harlequins in London, and would like to go. The hitch is that they are still under contract. Even though Dean Richards, the Harlequins' director, is prepared to pay out the contracts, Thierry wants to hold on to the players and won't let them go for anything. Fair enough—he is acting in what he thinks are the best interests of the club. Still, it's a shame for both of them. Dio, now 32, probably won't get another chance to move and it is a great opportunity for him. Clement is young enough, but he has recently broken up with his girlfriend, who works at the rugby club, so they still run into each other regularly and he could do with a change of scenery. He is one of those sturdy, uncomplaining soldiers you can see standing dutifully at the front of any battle line, and it would be good to see him get a break.

Toulon, when they arrive, are awful. They are missing a number of their more experienced players, have just changed coaches, and are dead last by a distance. They have nothing to play for, and away from their home turf they just aren't interested. Their line-out is shoddy, their scrum is in reverse, and to some extent it is a credit to them that they manage to hold out for 20 minutes before we cross their line, although David Bortolussi has already slotted a couple of penalties. When we do cross, however, the floodgates open, and it's 27–0 at half-time, before turning into a full-scale rout in the second half. We do well to keep our shape sufficiently to pile on the points, and the final score, 65–0, reflects the gulf between the two teams.

Just to keep things interesting, though, Pau beat Perpignan. After their victory in Toulon the week before, this puts them on 34 points, still in thirteenth place. We are in eleventh place on 40, with Bayonne on 37.

What makes the final straight particularly tasty is that we now go to Perpignan, play Agen at home (Agen are on fire at the moment, having beaten Castres in Castres the week before, and look like qualifying for the European Cup, so they will have everything to play for), then Biarritz, and finish with a home game against Stade Français. Three probable semifinalists, and one European contender: we should win at least one of these games, but we may not win any. If this happens and Pau win two, they will be ahead of us. Bloody Pau—they've had their heads under water so long you would have thought they'd have the decency to be dead by now, but I'm beginning to wonder whether they might do Glenn Close's bunny-boiler trick in *Fatal Attraction* and come screaming out of the bath with a knife.

The brighter news is that the win against Toulon has resulted in a cash bonus. After the game against Bourgoin, Thierry Pérez calculated that 19 more points should mean we were safe, and put up €100,000 for the players to divide among ourselves should we score 19 points over the coming six matches, which we have now done. It is ironic that we're not yet safe, but obviously Thierry can't go back on his word, so all we have to do now is work out how to divvy up a hundred grand. I suggest we establish a tradition whereby we give it all to the guys who are retiring (that is, me) as a golden handshake. Unfortunately, everyone seems to think that I'm joking.

I have had a hell of a time deciding whether I want to keep playing. At some point it was suggested that, given the club's key role in the process, I ask them whether they are at least interested in offering me a contract for another year. When I approached Nourault—who has jockeyed his way back into a good position for next season and will probably end up coaching again—his response was on the cool side of luke-warm. I gathered it was not likely to get any hotter. A well-mannered guest knows when to leave and so I will make my exit with dignity, at about the exact moment that the door gets slammed in my face.

Going the Distance

We go to Perpignan for our return match at the end of April, when the championship is getting close to delivering its verdict. Perpignan are almost certain to play the semis, while we are still holding out in eleventh place but feeling the heat. We have little hope of winning, but a bonus point at this stage would be very useful.

I'm on the bench, and now we're here I'm not terribly unhappy about it. It will be a hard game, and aged thirty-four there is no use kidding myself: I haven't played enough rugby over the last few weeks to be competitive against a top side for more than half a game.

Nourault's pre-match speech annoys me. He talks about it being a 'must-win game', which we all know it's not; next week against Agen at home will be a genuine must-win. You can only say you're playing must-win games and then go and lose them a certain number of times before the concept becomes meaningless. He follows this by saying, '*On a rien à leur envier*—essentially 'They are no better than we are'—which just shows a lack of humility as Perpignan are placed third on 69, while we are eleventh on 40. Of course they're better than we are. There must be something more constructive to say. Why can't we talk tactics, or at least have something genuinely motivational? The players are rolling their eyes at each other, and not for the first time I decide that Nourault has run out of steam.

As is often the case, Pat Arlettaz speaks after him and finds the right tone. He used to play for Perpignan himself and knows what a cauldron we are about to be thrown into. He talks about the pride and the culture, and the influence that the Catalan crowd seem to have on the game, and points out that this is simply background noise—the quality of a team's spirit comes from the inside, and we have our own strengths we can rely on.

It is a funny feeling going into a stadium where I have been so many times before and then not turning left to go into the home changing-room, but turning right and walking down the corridor to the visitors'. It is not the first time I've been back: the year after I left we played well and lost narrowly. Despite being booed when I held up play for a couple of minutes because I couldn't get a contact lens back in, I received an ovation from the crowd at the end of the game. I got a little misty about it: it's good to feel appreciated.

Although Perpignan supporters are famously one-eyed, they don't follow their team blindly. If they feel the players are not giving it their all, they will let them know, and are not afraid to boo them if they think the occasion calls for it. I once returned after a 40-odd point away loss against Stade Français to find a note on my car: 'Shame on you all! What must the Catalans who live in Paris have thought?'

As we check out the pitch beforehand I run into a few Perpignan players I know. It's good to see them. To be honest, I can't help feeling jealous. I know they will be thinking to themselves, 'This might be sticky for a while, but we will win.' At least, that's what I used to do when I was there. This may sound complacent, but it's not: it's just the confidence in your own abilities and those of your team-mates that comes from success. At Montpellier we have done some good things, but we have been conscious of the sword of Damocles hanging over our heads, and knowing the least slip can lead to disaster is stressful and prevents you getting into a rhythm.

When I came to Perpignan after playing for Racing, I felt as though I had started going out with a celebrity. Intrinsically you are the same person, but overnight you are transformed from a nonentity into someone of interest because everyone is watching. I have played in front of bigger crowds than the 14,000 who pack themselves into Stade Aimé Giral, but they have never made the hairs stand up on the back of my neck the way the roar of the crowd does when you come out of the tunnel here. After experiencing the unbelievably enthusiastic support of the Catalans, Montpellier felt a bit of a comedown.

The game starts in extraordinary fashion when Laurent Arbo burgles an intercept and scores before a minute is up on the clock. Nearly a quarter of an hour passes before Perpignan reply with a try from Manas: 5–5. The tit-for-tat session continues. Julien Laharrague drops a goal for them, Régis Lespinas drops one for us; Guillaume Bortolaso scores for them and Mathieu Bourret converts; Seb Kuzbik scores for us and David Aucagne converts. Unfortunately, the symmetry is broken when Laharrague scores a try and Bourret converts with ten minutes to go—we don't 'tat' their 'tit' and at half-time we are down 15–22.

In the first quarter of an hour of the second half they put the result out of our reach, having no doubt been reminded, during the team talk at the break, of what had happened in Montpellier. (What we thought of as our glorious comeback, they perceived as their collapse.) Their young kicker Mathieu Bourret slots a penalty, Nicolas Mas scores a try, then Greg Le Corvec scores another, which Bourret converts, and suddenly it's 15–37 and could easily hit 50.

With just over 20 minutes to go I come off the bench, at the same time as Perpignan's former All Black Scott 'Razor' Robertson. I hurtle around trying to be useful. After a few minutes I run into Razor in a ruck and he says, 'Jesus, you've got another three years in you,' which we both know is a lie, but it's nice to hear from an All Black and my ego needs massaging today. A few minutes later Perpignan push us off our own ball at the scrum, and run a simple move on the short side for Jean-Philippe Grandclaude to score: 15–42.

They have now scored six tries; their five-point haul for the victory, plus attacking bonus, is assured, and they take their foot slightly off the throat. We react well. We have quite a lot of ball now but are having trouble breaking through their defensive lines, so Coco puts a clever little kick in behind them and Seb Logerot scores in the corner. That makes it three tries for us, and with quarter of an hour to go there is a real possibility we may pocket the attacking bonus ourselves if we can score again.

But if Perpignan are not that bothered about increasing their tally, they are proud enough not to want us to score. Their defence allows itself the luxury of giving penalties away: they know we want the try and three points is no use to us. So we go to line-outs deep in their 22 again and again, and every time they step across into the gap and disrupt our jumpers, making it impossible to get the clean ball we need to set up a maul. It's very frustrating, but I have to admit that it is cleverly done: they manage to get their jumpers up at the same time so it looks reasonably legitimate, and the referee lets them get away with it.

We should probably belt them to discourage the practice, but you need to feel very punchy to start laying about you at Aimé Giral. And besides, we are convinced that we can score a try if we just get one clean ball. But it's too scrappy, there's no platform, and they are killing even our ruck ball.

At one point Colin Gaston, who has been a pain in the arse all afternoon, leaves his long legs poking through to our side as he lies under a pile-up, and kicks the ball just as Seb Galtier goes to pick it up. The referee whistles for a knock-on against us. Seb jumps on Gaston's legs in frustration, the two packs square up, and for a moment it looks as though a brawl is finally going to kick off, but no one is willing to put the flame to the tinderbox. In the end they hold out (or we miss out, depending on your point of view), so we are left hoping we won't end up ruing another lost opportunity to garner a point.

After the game I am looking forward to catching up with the Perpignan players, but I find that Montpellier are eating apart, consigned to the club-rooms of the *école de rugby*, just behind the main stand. Perpignan is the only club in the first division where this happens. It is a shame. As Serge Simon, a former French prop who is now president of the players' union, once said of rugby: '*C'est un jeu ou on peut se mettre des marrons et puis aller boire des bières ensemble après*'—'It's a game where we can slap each other around and then go and have a beer together afterwards.' These days, given the high stakes of professionalism, it is less easy to wind down than it used to be, and relations between opposing teams are also less convivial. Even so, most players know each other by name and there is a mutual respect that develops; getting to know opposing players after a game is part of the camaraderie.

The argument against it is, of course, economic. The Perpignan players need to eat in the same room as the club's sponsors so that the people who put the money into the club get some face-to-face contact time with the people they are effectively paying. The more sponsors the club can get into the room the better, and opposition players would just take up space where there would otherwise be paying customers. In certain circumstances it is worthwhile cramming the other team in. In Perpignan, Biarritz, for example, eat with the sponsors, because Biarritz have plenty of famous international players, and the sponsors get to rub shoulders with the stars. Lowly Montpellier have no shoulders worth rubbing, so we get shunted off backstage like the hired help—which, in a sense, we are.

The home game against Agen is crucial. We are now so close to the end of the season that we will have little chance to redeem ourselves if we make a mistake and the other teams take their opportunities. The relegation battle has become three-sided: Bayonne are behind us on 37, and Pau behind them on 34. We appear to be in the most comfortable position on 40 points, but after Agen we play away to Biarritz and then at home to Stade Français.

Both teams will be peaking, as we play them the week before they play crucial matches. A coincidence of the calendar means that while we are playing Agen, Pau are playing Biarritz at home, while Bayonne host Stade Français. Biarritz play the final of the European Cup in two weeks' time, so they are resting some key players, while a few others are on the bench. They don't need the points as they have already qualified for the semifinals. There is also a suggestion that they wouldn't be unhappy to see Pau stay up ahead of Bayonne; geographically speaking, Biarritz and Bayonne are virtually the same town, but when it comes to rugby they have a not very friendly rivalry.

Fortunately for Bayonne, Stade Français have also decided to rest a few players, which evens things up, but again, could make things uncomfortable for us: both Pau and Bayonne are unlikely to win their next round games, which are away, but the last round will see them at home against Castres and Montferrand respectively, and they may well win. Luckily, Agen have also decided to send out a mixed bag. A good performance should see us win, and that would put us out of danger.

I am slated to be on the bench, which suits me well enough. This season is the first when I have spent so much time as a reserve, and if it was initially hard to swallow I am now used to it and looking forward to the game. However, as we arrive at training I do a head count and realise there are too many players. There should be 24 of us, but I make it 25. Montpellier always carries two additional, non-playing reserves, invariably a front-rower and a utility back, in case someone breaks down at the last minute. I used to think this was unnecessary, but it is surprising the number of times they are used. Jérôme Vallée has been out with an injury for some time, but he is hoping to play. Jharay Russell and Seb Galtier are there as well, which is one more back-row reserve than we need, but if Nourault thinks he is taking a risk by starting Jérôme, perhaps he will cover two back-row slots and use Michel, who is playing number 8, as the lock reserve. This will mean I get the flick.

As we are warming up, Nourault calls me over. He starts in by saying that he has decided to play Jérôme, but I know what's coming next, and walk away before he has time to finish explaining. I could probably have handled this if Jérôme were at peak form, or there was another reason that I felt justified his selection, but we have been doing all right recently without him, he hasn't played for weeks, is carrying a back injury, and there are other guys capable of assuming his role. And provided we win this will be the last important match of the season—and of my career. The last two will just be runarounds. Fuck it. That, gentle reader, is professional rugby for you.

After this little drama, and high stakes in the build-up, the game itself is an anticlimax. We are wound up for a battle royal, but most of Agen's heavy artillery are at home or warming the reserve bench. Philemon bowls over a few players for a brace of tries in the first few minutes, David Bortolussi converts both and then adds a penalty on the quarter-hour mark, and Alex Stoica scores a couple of minutes later. With the game not yet half an hour old, Lolo Arbo scores to make it four tries, Bortolussi converts, it's 29–0 and the season is effectively over. They won't come back from this, and we have a five-point victory.

Just to make sure, Antony Vigna also scores, and Bortolussi converts again. At half-time it is 36–0, and Agen still haven't fired a shot. After making a few changes in the second half, they score three tries, but by then it's too late, and we round it off with a converted penalty try to make the score 44–19. Both Pau and Bayonne win as well, so mathematically we can't be sure we are saved, but Pau are playing Stade Français in Paris next weekend and they have no chance of winning there, especially after the Parisians lost in Bayonne.

Biarritz lies about 600 kilometres from Montpellier in the Basque country on the Atlantic coast. The long bus ride takes it out of us and claims one victim: Martin Durand has a niggle in his back flare up after more than six hours of travel, and by the time we arrive he is unable to play. I don't feel too flash myself, having acquired something resembling a groin strain after getting up from my usual position on the floor of the bus. (Trying to squeeze my two-metre frame into a bus seat is like squaring the circle, and I prefer to stretch out in the corridor, even though it means I collect an occasional shoe in the face.) Hell, if I can't even take a bus ride without injuring myself, it really is time to hang up my boots. Happily, it warms up all right at training and shouldn't bother me the next day.

Meanwhile, though, I am rooming with Antony Vigna, which is something of a disaster. Nearly all rugby players snore—most have broken noses—but Antony is a stand-out performer, with a strong deep roar interspersed with snuffling noises. When he was playing for Grenoble he was the only player allowed a room of his own, having been boycotted by the rest of the team. It's not the first time we have been lumped together so I know what's coming, and in my panic to get to sleep before he does I get myself so worked up the opposite occurs: when he starts his hibernating bear routine I am wide awake.

My grogginess the next day fits right in with the mood of the team. As we are now saved from relegation we have little to play for, and the pre-match team talk is full of ominous signs. Thierry Pérez asks us to *éviter le ridicule*—avoid being ridiculous—and Pat Arlettaz stoops to the old 'pride in the jersey' motivational speech. The idea of a bonus point is vaguely referred to but no one dwells on it.

Biarritz are using the game as a dress rehearsal for the European Cup final next week, so they have put out their top team. There is the slight hope that they may be worried about getting injured and therefore be tentative in contact, but they are too good for that: everyone knows that going into contact half-heartedly is, paradoxically, the best way to get injured. There is also the fact that one of our two away wins over the last couple of years was here, the week after they played the semifinal of the European Cup, but they put out a largely second-string side that day and are clearly not going to make the same mistake again. They are winding up, while we are winding down. We know it isn't going to be pretty.

And it isn't. Small-scale cock-ups that we might normally get away with are ruthlessly exploited, and the points pile up at an alarming rate. Twice, Michel calls throws to the back of the line-out, but he is shouting to Nico Grelon who is throwing in at the front; he doesn't take his mouth-guard out, the Biarritz crowd is singing, and the guys at the tail are surprised when the ball goes sailing over their head into open space because they haven't jumped. On both occasions Biarritz gather quickly, send it wide, keep the ball alive well, and score.

At one point we kick deep and arrive for the line-out. As we are organising ourselves they take a quick throw-in and their scrum-half, Dimitri Yachvili, romps 60 metres down the sideline to score. We look ridiculous but feel we are again getting a raw deal from the referee: on this occasion the line-out shouldn't have been allowed to be taken quickly because it was already formed. Heads go down or start yapping. Seb

Petit, our prop, takes it a step too far and gets a yellow card for questioning the referee's eyesight.

Despite a high tolerance level for occasional mistakes by the ref, I am also starting to feel frustrated. Towards the end of the first half, Biarritz chip a kick through a little too far and we are able to touch down in goal. I am standing on the 22-metre line, and there is a big hole in front of me. I am passed the ball, and as I bend down to do a sneaky little quick drop out to myself, I get cut in half by Serge Betsen, who arrives from behind me. Obviously he is offside and shouldn't have tackled me, so as I pick myself up I ask the referee, who is allowing play to continue, where the Biarritz flanker might have appeared from if he wasn't offside. Whistle. Penalty against my big mouth. Biarritz kick to touch, take the ball cleanly and start mauling slowly towards the tryline. I go to pull down the maul—legal if you are the first man in defence, and something I usually do quite well—but find they are so compact and well-structured that the bastards won't go down, and they score again.

They are a bloody good side. Things are going so fast I have lost count, but at half-time the scoreboard shows that they have scored six tries and are winning 43–0. (A few weeks later I will find it reassuring to watch them put 31 points, including five tries, on Toulouse in the second half of the final, which they win 40–13.)

They go a bit easier on us in the second half, bringing on reserves. I limit myself to a couple of well-chosen epithets directed at the ref, and save my breath for the running around: I haven't played the full 80 minutes for months and am not finding it easy. After they score their first try of the second half—about 20 minutes in—I go up to compete for a kick-off with Jérôme Thion. However, with his lifters under him he gets high, while I, knackered and operating under my own steam, barely get off the ground. My shoulder hits his rear, he hurtles to the ground, and as I fall I reach out and grab at him in a reflex action that makes his crash to the floor even uglier. Oops. I would feel very bad if he couldn't play the final next week because of me. The Biarritz forwards close in, but I think they can see that I am genuinely worried and that it wasn't deliberate. Thion, swearing, lies motionless for a while, but I drag him to his feet and luckily he stays up without further assistance.

After the game I feel low with accumulated fatigue and the heavy defeat. I have had a few hidings in my life but it is a while since I had 50 points put past me. Strangely enough, I feel I played all right: despite giving away a couple of penalties, I took the ball up about a dozen times without losing it, made a few good tackles, including one covering tackle on Thion that was enough of a thump to make him spill the ball forward, and my tight work wasn't too bad, even if I wasn't able to stop their maul from scoring. Normally, this would be enough for me to say that it wasn't my problem, the fault lay somewhere else and at least I had done my job. But this time, it isn't. At the after-match I am still pulling myself together. I darkly note that some match officials are laughing, joking and having their photographs taken with the Biarritz players.

The Slippery Slope

Stade Français have built a reputation for doing things a little differently. An example came under Nick Mallett. When the club reached the middle of the winter without being as well-placed as they would have liked, a break in the championship for the Six Nations meant they had a week without a game. Mallett might easily have used this as a training camp to try to whip them into shape after a disappointing start to the season. Instead, the South African took his troops off to the alps for a few days skiing, far from the muddy, and occasionally frozen, training grounds of the capital. Some skiing went on—by all accounts there was quite a bit of *apres-ski* as well—but Mallett let the team get on with pretty much whatever they felt like. Some observers—and even, I think, some of the team—thought this was crazy, but Mallett had read the situation brilliantly. The players came back refreshed and ready for the business end of the season, and went on to win the championship.

When rugby went professional, players could spend more time training, and this led to an improvement in player skills and levels of physical preparation. In addition, clubs became employers, rather than people organising what you did for fun, and because they were paying they wanted to see you sweat. This was fair enough, and by and large standards of play have risen considerably. However, if your work ethic is telling you that to get an edge you will have to train relentlessly—more than the other guys—the positive effects of repetition can easily slip into overkill: everyone else is working hard, and to do more than them you have to do a hell of a lot. Quite quickly, something you once enjoyed can make you wonder whether you want to get out of bed in the morning.

Enthusiasm is one of the keys to playing well, and if spending a week skiing allows a team to bond in a healthy way and forget about scrums and line-outs and rucking and mauling and tackling and catching and passing and kicking and all the rest of their normal activities, and they are mature enough to use the time to recharge their batteries, it is worth doing.

Enthusiasm is easy to have when you're young and recovering quickly. As the years wear on, rugby takes a toll on your body and, up to a point, your mind. Having to worry about creaking knees, a sore back, and that shoulder niggle that just won't go away, takes some of the shine off your enjoyment, even if it doesn't affect your determination.

And enthusiasm goes hand in hand with confidence, which is a massively important part of a player's mental ability.

When I was about twenty, having played for the New Zealand Colts I considered myself an All Black-in-waiting: it was just a matter of time, I thought, before I would be one of the world's best players. I was already in the ante-room. Now that I have played a couple of hundred first-class games and never got within shouting distance of an All Black jersey, this attitude strikes me as seriously deluded, but at the time it was a major asset. Going on to the field believing you are better than the other guy gives you a massive head start. Such confidence can't last, obviously, but while it does you are hard to beat.

When eventually you have to come to terms with the fact that there are people out there who are at least as good as you, and perhaps quite a bit better, it's character-building, but it isn't necessarily a good thing for your game. Instead of going out saying to yourself that you are going to prove you are better than the guy opposite, you wonder how good he is, and all the little things that may go wrong crowd into your consciousness. One of the hardest, but most vital, things in sport is to learn how to lose from time to time. All the things you thought made you so good have to be re-examined, and your failings identified and broken down. Only then can you build yourself back up to become a better player.

People find their confidence in different ways, and humility is good protection from falling too far, but if you want to compete with the best you have to rate yourself highly, and this means treading a fine line between confidence and arrogance—not swaggering around as though you own the place, but having faith in your ability to come out ahead of the other guy. The margin between individuals at the top level of most sports is very small. In a 100-metre final, all runners will probably finish within one or two metres of their competitors and it will be the one who gets his or her nose in front who wins. What is going on in your head can make all the difference.

Ending up with a big ego is rare in rugby, as in most team sports, because you are surrounded by fellow players who will let you know if you have an inflated idea of yourself. Commanders of Roman armies were allowed to parade through the streets of Rome after victorious campaigns, but the senate ensured that they had someone alongside them in the chariot to whisper in their ear, '*Memento mori*' ('Remember you will die'). At the end of the English season, just before our return game against Stade Français, Jonny Wilkinson comes down to stay with Harley Crane—they used to play at Newcastle together. Wilkinson may be the highest paid player in world rugby, and the man who won the World Cup for England, but he still has to deal with Crano relentlessly roasting him about his dodgy haircut.

Mental maturity is supposed to come with experience, and French clubs tend to value experience over youth, often buying in older foreign players rather than giving younger home-grown ones a chance; there's a feeling that young players need to prove themselves over a number of seasons at lower levels. In New Zealand the attitude is quite different: if you're good enough, you're old enough. Indeed, thirty is considered the start of the downhill run, while in France there are plenty of players in their early thirties who are considered to be at their peak. The average age of the All Blacks' 2006 squad was 25.5, while for the French Six Nations squad it was 28.5.

I have personally benefited from the French emphasis on experience, but its importance may be an illusion: once a player has mastered the fundamentals, rugby is not very complicated. If you can handle the jump to a higher level, you will come into contact with better players and progress quickly. And often the younger you are, the more quickly you adapt. This year in Montpellier we have had the example of Fulgence ('Fufu') Ouedraogo, who has improved so dramatically at the age of twenty that, having started the season in the *Espoirs*, he is now one of our best players.

This is good news for the club, but fairly average news for the other flankers: as we are ringing the changes, some are on the way out. During one of the particularly flat training sessions we have before the last game against Stade Français, Didier Bes and Thierry Pérez have a long conversation on the sideline. Judging by Didier's sharp-edged gesticulations and Thierry's stony face, it doesn't look good for Didier, and during the period between the end of this season and the start of the next he is shunted off to coach the Reichels, the Under 21 piranhas. This is hard on him: the forwards have been solid in his domain of scrums and line-outs all year. If anything, it's been one of our strengths.

Meanwhile, Thierry announces that Nourault is staying on. Jérôme has earlier organised a 'democratic' vote on whether Nourault should coach us next season. The result was massively against, but Thierry has made his decision.

Alain Hyardet is confirmed as the replacement for Pat Arlettaz as backs' coach. Olivier Sarraméa from Stade Français,
Argentinian Federico Todeschini from Béziers and Didier
Chouchan from Biarritz are confirmed as new recruits. Again,
this is good news for the club because they are good players,
but less good news for the people whose places they will no
doubt occupy, and there are one or two long faces when we
hear the news.

The Georgian Mamuka Magrakvelidze has not had his
contract renewed, and our fullback Fred Benazech has been
'let go', despite having another year on his contract. Everyone else will be back again to start pre-season in just over a
month.

Except me, of course. As I go into what will be my last game
of rugby I find myself unable to take in the enormity of the
fact that, after 25 years, I won't be doing this again. This is
coupled with the unpleasant realisation that I now have to
find a 'real' job. Professional rugby looks a sweet deal when
you are in your early twenties, and your non-rugby-playing
friends are struggling to find work, or starting at the bottom
of a career ladder. However, now I am in my early thirties and
my friends have managed to work their way up the career
ladder, I am the one who has to start at the bottom.

In the changing-room before the game, I try to drink in the
atmosphere and ignore the void that lies ahead, but idle
thoughts drift across my mind. I wonder whether I should go
and have a massage. Lots of players do, but I have always
thought it would send me to sleep so I've never bothered.

Now I'll never have the chance again. And it's free. Christ, I'm going to start having to pay if I want to go to the gym.

Come on, concentrate. You need to play well, to finish on a good note. I visualise things I will be doing in the game, make sure I have a mental image of doing them well, and busy myself with my boots. We go out to warm up, and I am reminded of how hot it is. All the games are being played at the same time, three o'clock on Saturday afternoon, so that no club has an advantage, but summer starts early in the south of France, and already it is well over 30 degrees.

After the warm-up we come back into the changing-room and pour water over ourselves in an attempt to cool down. Then we make our usual preparations. In my case it's Vaseline on the ears, Vicks VapoRub under the nose, and a strap around my left wrist to prevent the bone popping out. We huddle together for a few final words. It seems so unreal I can't register what is said.

Fred Benazech and I lead the team out with our arms around each other. We have played together for two seasons but it is only in the last couple of weeks that I have started to understand him. I have heard that at the Agen game he was misty-eyed in the changing-room: he had just that week heard the club wouldn't be keeping him on.

I had always thought Fred wasn't really interested in excelling. I once heard him greeted by a journalist as 'the greatest waste of talent in French rugby', which he seemed to take as a compliment. I have seen him throw out of the back of his hand, behind his own goal-line, a suicidal 30-yard reverse pass that was intercepted and a seven-point gift to the opposition, but I have also seen him run a ball back from 70 yards out through most of the opposing team and score an amazing individual try.

It's not, I've come to realise, that he's not interested: he has just held on to the simple joy of risk-taking, and rates this above playing a dour, safe percentage game. This is what commentators mean when they talk about French flair, and you don't see much of it these days. Playing this kind of game matters to him enough that, although he's nearly the same age as I am, he is going to play another year of rugby with a third-division club.

Determined to do something impressive in my last game, I run around like a rookie, and when a break in play allows me to look at the clock I see there are only seven minutes gone. How am I going to make it to half-time in this heat? The Parisians, seeing the game as a dress rehearsal for next week's semifinal, have their best side out and are in impressive form, while we are mentally at the beach having barbecues.

A couple of minutes later Fred goes off injured. It's still nil all, but it won't stay that way for long. We are using up a massive amount of energy just to hold on to our own ball. Scrums are such a struggle that after a couple, despite knowing I am needed at the next phase, I lurk on the wing, knackered, until I can catch my breath. I take up the ball a few times and have a hell of a time holding on to it in contact. Stade Française are in like robbers' dogs, low, strong and very hard to shift, and once I am penalised for not releasing.

After 20 minutes Skrela kicks a penalty. This is a turning point: Stade Français score twice in quick succession, and after 25 minutes the score is 0–15. They dominate every phase of play. I manage to pull down a couple of their mauls, but when I miss one they roll right over the top of me, and unlike the gentlemanly Biarritz pack, they really work me over, deliberately targeting weak points. Knees and ankle joints, where there is less flesh, are vulnerable, and even though I am wearing shin-pads my lower legs begin to look like as though someone has been playing noughts and crosses on them with a knife.

With five minutes to the break, David Bortolussi dots down for us to make it 5–15, but Stade Français score again, and then convert to make it 5–22. At half-time, as we are dousing ourselves again, it occurs to me that people die from heatstroke in conditions like these. How long will I have to stay on before Nourault pulls me off?

One of the big differences between the two teams is that we go to ground and waste time and energy having to recycle the ball, while Stade Français keep it alive, making passes out of contact situations. Partly this is because their players have good individual skills, but it's also because we haven't placed enough emphasis in training on passing in the contact zone. Hopefully, the lesson will be learned for next year.

I leave the field, mercifully, just ten minutes into the second half. Stade Français score again to put the game beyond any lingering doubt at 5–29, but then we manage a brace of rapid-fire tries, one by Régis Lespinas and another by Laurent Arbo, well set up by Seb Mercier, who shimmies through the opposition centres and runs 60 metres before offloading to Lolo. Just to drive the nail home, Stade

Français score another couple of tries, making it 17–43, but Lolo Arbo has the final word. As his second try is our fourth, we get a bonus point, making the whole thing look a little more respectable.

Meanwhile, Pau and Bayonne both lose their games, so Pau finish on 40 points and go down, while Bayonne end up on 43, us on 46 and Narbonne on 47. Castres, on 66, head off Montferrand, on 63, to qualify for the European Cup next season.

Ideally, the last game of a career would be one in which your team wins the championship, or at least the game, but I manage to convince myself the result was a good one for me because, coming on the heels of the Biarritz game, it convinced me I no longer have what it takes to compete at the top level. Against anyone other than the big three, I think I still hold my own (a bit like Montpellier), and were I to be lucky enough to be playing in one of these teams I might be carried for another season. But there is no room for margin of error in a small club. I might be able to find another club that needed someone like me, but it would probably be in the second division, and I don't want to spend another season just hanging on. As it is, my body has been giving me warning signs most of this year.

Despite being hammered, we do a little run round the pitch—not so much a victory lap as a 'we're still here' lap—clapping the supporters and being clapped by them. Nico Grelon and Philemon Toleafoa hoist me up on their shoulders, and I perch uncomfortably for about ten yards before

Nico says, '*Putain, il est lourd, l'ancien*' ('Fuck, the old man is heavy') and they put me down.

As the old man of Montpellier, I am intensely aware of how the game has changed since I was a young player. When I played my first game for Wellington in 1994, lifting in the line-out was still outlawed, tries had been worth five points for only a couple of years, and flankers could break off the side of the scrum. I remember this particularly because I was considered mobile enough in those days to be stuck on the flank, and for that first game, against Auckland, I had to cope with an All Black back row of Zinzan Brooke, Michael Jones and Mark Carter. Most of the time I hovered about a metre off the scrum, terrified they would rumble my cart-horse speed off the mark. All I got from the game was a ticket so my Mum could watch from the stands, and a memory that I plan to take with me to the grave.

Just a few years later I was heading back to Paris with Racing Club. We had won the semifinal that meant we qualified to go up to the first division. As we were celebrating we called the club president, Gerald Martinez, down to the back of the bus. He arrived with a big grin, certain we were going to get him involved in drinking games or similar mischief. In fact, we asked him for a bonus. The grin crumpled.

It would be hypocritical of me, one of the first wave of rugby's international mercenaries, to mourn the passing of the amateur era. I am grateful to have had the opportunity to make money out of what I enjoy doing. But I can't help hoping that rugby doesn't become a multinational corporation and lose its human touch. Winston Churchill once said,

'We make a living by what we get; we make a life by what we give.' In the years to come, I hope that rugby players—amateurs, professionals and mercenaries—make sure they give at least as good as they get.

Epilogue

A year on, the club game in France continues to attract growing interest from all quarters. Average match attendances have passed the 10,000 mark, while television rights for the Top 14 and the Second Division (Pro D2) have been renegotiated at €117 million (more than NZ$200 million) over the next four years, an increase of 45 percent over the previous period. The economic benefits of this have fed through to the players: average pay in the Top 14 has risen another €12,000 a year. France is now more attractive than ever to the mercenary.

The arrival of several ultra-wealthy businessmen on the club scene has led to startling inflation at the top end of the market. Current All Blacks can now command an annual salary of over €250,000 after tax. From the end of October 2006 to the start of January 2007, the iconic Tana Umaga played a total of eight games for second-division Toulon, for which he received a reported €350,000. After the 2007

World Cup, Australia's George Gregan will go to Toulon for an estimated €400,000. Byron Kelleher has already signed with Toulouse. Victor Matlock and Stephen Larkham are said to be next on recruiters' lists.

The flip side of these huge pay-packets is the greater expectation that goes with them. Clubs and fans will want to see a return on investment. Tana Umaga set the bar very high at Toulon. Although the team underperformed most of the season and failed to win promotion to the first division, they won every game that Tana played, and the increase in gate takings more than paid for his transfer. But French rugby can still be a minefield, no matter how distinguished your career —just ask Daniel Herbert—and the super-recruits will need to perform. If they're planning on a few months wine-tasting in the south of France as they flick through their investment portfolios, they may be in for a nasty shock.

The effect of the latest player exodus on rugby in the southern hemisphere is yet to be seen, but alarm bells must be ringing in Wellington, Sydney and Cape Town. The simple fact of supply and demand, coupled with the financial gulf between the south and the north, may erode the traditional strength of the game in the south. A former senior NZRU official recently told me that, in the long term, New Zealand could be obliged to put in place a partnership system with big European clubs, and/or with the Japanese companies that run rugby in that country.

That is, unless the northern hemisphere unions decide to intervene. There are already rumblings in France about the number of foreigners in the French championship. Roughly a third of first-division players are from overseas, a figure many French officials consider excessive. European employment law would make it difficult to limit the number of foreigners playing in France, but the possibility of a mandatory number of French eligible players on a team sheet is being explored.

Meanwhile, Montpellier struggled through another year. With two games to play, my old club was second to last and everyone's pick to go down. A home game against Biarritz, the reigning champions, had us drinking in the last-chance saloon. After home losses against Perpignan, Montferrand and even Brive we looked unlikely to defy predictions, but in a stunning 39–29 upset Montpellier scored five tries to pocket the bonus along with the win, and get up to tenth place.

In the last round of the season six different teams—Agen, Albi (an unfancied but surprisingly successful team of battlers freshly up from the second division), Bayonne, Montpellier, Brive and Castres—could have joined Narbonne (dead last) in the second division. Montpellier played away to Perpignan, who needed a win with a bonus point to make it through to the semi-finals. Montpellier needed a win to be sure to stay up, but if one of the teams placed behind them lost, that would be enough.

With all the games kicking off at 5 p.m., Montpellier supporters watched their team with one ear stuck to the radio. After twenty minutes, Montpellier were losing and all the other candidates for the drop were winning. Second division here we come.

Then Stade Français, playing Agen in Agen, started to pull away from the locals. Agen had signed Byron Kelleher to a pre-contract and had played European Cup this year. Breathless, we waited for them to bounce back, but the gap kept getting bigger. Meanwhile Perpignan were beating Montpellier, but only just. Before the final whistle blew in Perpignan—14–9 to the home team—the result had come through from Agen: 18-6 to Stade Français. Montpellier would live to fight another day.

READ ABOUT RUGBY'S GREATEST CONTEST

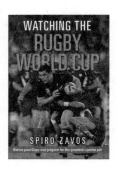

Watching the Rugby World Cup
SPIRO ZAVOS

'From one of the great rugby journalists, a superb book for those who love the sport, the drama, and the thrill of victory'
David Kirk

In 2007, 20 rugby-playing nations try and bring home rugby's most coveted prize, the William Webb Ellis trophy. Over 44 drama-filled days, supporters pour into stadiums in France, Scotland and Wales to watch 47 matches, culminating in the final in Paris. Around the globe, an estimated 3.4 billion television viewers take in the action.

In this book, Spiro Zavos writes of the events that, in just 20 years, have made the Rugby World Cup one of the world's top sporting contests, and provides a riveting guide to players, coaches, strategies and national styles. He also gives striking insight into rugby as it is played in France, the 2007 host country.

Spiro Zavos is recognised as one of the world's most influential rugby writers. As well as numerous articles in leading newspapers and magazines, he has written eight acclaimed books on rugby, has a long-running column in *The Sydney Morning Herald*, and is the author of the best-seller *How to Watch a Game of Rugby*.

'As comprehensive and entertaining a book on the World Cup as has ever been written'
Peter FitzSimons

Available from all good bookstores, or purchase online at

www.awapress.com

Awa Press
PO Box 11-416, Wellington 6142, New Zealand
Tel +64 4 385-0740   fax + 64 4 382-9032
Email sales@awapress.com

How to Catch a Cricket Match   HARRY RICKETTS

'Like the game itself, Ricketts casts an enchanting spell'

The New Zealand Herald

Rudyard Kipling called cricketers 'flannelled fools'. Groucho Marx asked halfway through a cricket match when it would begin. Alfred Hitchcock put two cricket fans into a thriller as comic relief. Yet despite its slow pace, strange language, eccentric umpires and frequent scandals – or perhaps *because* of them – cricket is today one of the world's most passionately followed and played sports. In New Zealand, watching a cricket match is the quintessence of summer, so when cricket-obsessed writer Harry Ricketts and his Australian friend Tony take themselves to the second day of a test against the West Indies, things are bound to start happening…

Harry Ricketts is a cricket buff, writer, poet, university lecturer, theatre critic, editor of *New Zealand Books*, and author of *The Unforgiving Minute: A Life of Rudyard Kipling*.

How to Catch a Fish   KEVIN IRELAND

'A small masterpiece. Oh, that all angling books were as pleasurable as this'

The Dominion Post

For Kevin Ireland, fishing – especially for the elusive trout – is not an idle pastime. It's a passionate love affair with the natural world. Since getting hooked as a boy, he has punted on wild Irish lakes, clambered over medieval abbeys, studied ancient Greek texts, chewed the fat with numerous other devotees, and spent several thousand hours actually fishing. This book, he says, is the sum total of all he now knows, or will ever know, about how to catch a fish. If you have ever dangled a line or cast with a rod, you will love this wise, warm and funny book.

Kevin Ireland is one of New Zealand's most acclaimed writers, winner of the Montana Award for History and Biography, the National Book Award for Poetry, and the Prime Minister's Award for Poetry.

For more titles in the Ginger Series, see www.awapress.com

SHARE THE PASSION FOR THE PERFECT GAME

How to Watch a Game of Rugby
SPIRO ZAVOS

'Wonderfully compelling – an entirely new approach to watching
the game'

Rugby News

Spiro Zavos, a first-generation Greek New Zealander, saw his first
rugby test when he was 12 years old and was struck with a lifelong
passion for 'the perfect game'. In this best-selling book, the
celebrated rugby writer sets out to convince readers that rugby is the
world's greatest sport.

Along the way he tackles some of the great mysteries: How *did*
England win the 2003 World Cup? Which US president played fullback
at Yale? And should players have sex before a match?

A book to enchant both keen rugby fans and those who don't know
a ruck from a maul – yet.

Spiro Zavos is an influential rugby writer, who has written eight
acclaimed books on the sport. His rugby column for *The Sydney
Morning Herald* has run for more than 20 years.

Available from all good bookstores, or purchase online at

www.awapress.com

Awa Press
PO Box 11-416, Wellington 6142, New Zealand
Tel +64 4 385-0740   fax + 64 4 382-9032
Email sales@awapress.com